T3-BPX-775

Regulation
of the Firm
and
Natural Monopoly

Regulation
of the Firm
and
Natural Monopoly

Michael Waterson

Basil Blackwell

Copyright © Michael Waterson 1988

First published 1988

Basil Blackwell Ltd
108 Cowley Road, Oxford, OX4 1JF, UK

Basil Blackwell Inc.
432 Park Avenue South, Suite 1503
New York, NY 10016, USA

British Library Cataloguing in Publication Data

Waterson, Michael
   Regulation of the firm and natural monopoly
   1. Industry and state   2. Trade regulation
   I. Title
   338.9′009181′2   HD3612

   ISBN 0-631-14007-7

Library of Congress Cataloging in Publication Data

Waterson, Michael. 1950–
   Regulation of the firm and natural monopoly.

   Bibliography: p.
   Includes index.
   1. Industry and state. 2. Industrial organization.
3. Monopolies. I. Title.
HD3611.W35 1988   338.8   87-20925
ISBN 0-631-14007-7

Typeset in 10½/12 pt Times
by MHL Typesetting Ltd, Coventry
Printed in Great Britain by TJ Press, Padstow

Contents

Preface

The current debate about regulation is most probably unparalleled in its scope and geographical coverage. Old assumptions are being questioned, and new policies proposed, throughout a very large section of the Western world, involving industries that account for substantial proportions of GNP. This trend emanates partly from the gut feelings of its proponents, partly from political considerations and partly from economics. It would be natural for an economist to argue that the last of these is the most important. Moreover, few economists would say that the economic arguments are unambiguous. Hence the rationale for this book, as a theoretical, and to a lesser extent an empirical, exploration of this debate from an economic standpoint.

Naturally enough, the economic debate has been fuelled by a considerable, and continually growing, amount of material. This book aims to provide some form of digest of this material, accessible to final year undergraduates. The intention has been to focus upon the arguments in a dispassionate manner and thus to step back somewhat from current debates in pursuing the analysis. These therefore are not introduced until late into the text. To this extent at least the book differs from some, though undoubtedly not all, similar studies.

Much of the argument in the book is verbal and diagrammatic, although a limited amount of mathematics is used. In order to appreciate the analysis, it would be useful for the reader to have an elementary knowledge of calculus up to the Lagrangean multiplier technique, and in addition some familiarity with the more usual and straightforward concepts of industrial economics. Most of the material, however, will be accessible to any final year economics student.

It would be remiss of me not to acknowledge the help I have had from various people in writing this book. In particular, the publisher's readers, Steve Davies and, in the earlier stages, Richard Schmalensee, were very useful (in both cases, the cloak of anonymity quickly wore rather thin!). Steve Davies has undoubtedly helped to make it a much better book than it would otherwise have been. Others who have read and commented upon

Preface

shorter portions of the book include Brian Beavis, James Foreman-Peck, Ian Molho, Virginie Perotin and Norman Strong. Though I have tended to take (my version of) their advice, none of the above should be held responsible for errors or omissions in the final product.

Finally, I must acknowledge the help of Sue Corbett and Paul Dutton, from Basil Blackwell, who bullied me in sequence into producing the material.

M.W.

1

The Meaning and Purpose of Regulation

Economic regulation might be defined broadly as government interference in what could be a market-based activity. So why does government interfere? In this book I pose and try to answer three questions:

1 For what *reasons* does government choose to regulate certain industries?
2 Is there a *legitimate economic rationale* for such regulation?
3 On balance, does regulation work?

Being a study in economics, the book focuses on the latter two questions.

1.1 An outline

Later in the chapter I provide a framework indicating how the form of regulation we shall discuss — sometimes called 'economic regulation' — relates to certain other types. First though, by way of an overview, let us consider the parties involved. By definition, regulation implies there are regulators, presumably governmental agents. They attempt to impose their will on the firm(s) involved, that influence extending perhaps to deciding on *who* may be involved. To take an example from a related sphere, in regulating credit brokers, controls are imposed on firms in the industry, and conditions must be met by those intending to enter this line of business. Thus the nature of the existing industry is considered important, as well as the nature of the would-be entrant firm.

Given that we are limiting our discussion to industries where competition is problematic, the extent of natural competition is fundamental. This topic is examined in the next chapter, along with important questions of how production can, and how it might best be, funded in such circumstances. Having seen that there is an a priori case for some governmental interference, we will pass on in chapter 3 to applications of the theory of the firm to regulated situations — how we might expect such firms to behave. Chapters 4 and 5 analyse in greater depth two common alternative regulatory frameworks, state control and rate regulation, building upon the early material. A third, less common, alternative is covered in chapter 6. This involves stratagems for introducing competition where none may exist.

Regulation can have potential societal benefits, as I shall demonstrate below and in more detail in chapter 2. Unfortunately it also has (actual and) potential social costs. This brings us to the third question: is regulation worthwhile? This is a question first of whether some forms of regulatory frameworks are superior to others and then of whether *any* form of regulation is worthwhile. It is in large part an empirical question, and issues and studies bearing on the topic are considered in chapter 7. Chapter 8 provides a brief overview and conclusion.

This still leaves the first topic, namely why in practice government does interfere, and the question of motivations embodied in one central group of actors not so far highlighted, the regulators themselves. The first part of this is a more general political question which cannot be covered fully in an economics text. However, both this question and the regulators themselves have received attention in the economics literature and this material is treated in section 1.3 below. Before that, we must first delimit the area we are to consider.

1.2   What is meant by 'economic regulation'?

Regulation here is taken as meaning control of an industrial activity by government, in the sense of actions such as restrictions on firms entering the industry, constraints on firms actually in the industry, or both. We might add to these, government powers affecting substitutes and complements and direct subsidizing of activities. Even then, there are numerous examples to choose as illustrations of regulated industries: the postal service, electricity distribution, taxi services, opticians, asbestos manufacturing. These have little in common with one another, but they do illustrate particular facets of (potential) competitive market failure.

The great claim made for perfect competition is that it leads to efficiency. Therefore *if* efficiency is a prime goal at which to aim, why not simply allow competition to do the job? Logically, there are three possibilities which may counsel caution. First, in some areas of activity there may be no competition, or even no potential competition. Secondly, competition may exist but, because there are some problems with the actors or actions involved, efficient results may be undesirable. Efficiency need not be the only goal. Thirdly, competition may exist but, because some assumptions are violated, the automatic link with efficiency is broken.

Our concern essentially is with the first of these possibilities, the case of natural monopoly — no competition is possible. At the moment, I will be fairly casual about what is meant by 'natural monopoly', because the matter is covered in detail in chapter 2. But, loosely, some industries, such as letter post, water supply and electricity supply, appear to be cases where extensive and extended competition is not the norm, and where such competition may indeed be wasteful. What can, or should, be done in such cases?

Notice first that I have implied a tradeoff, which should be made more explicit and later will be explored in additional detail. Competition is sometimes possible: two firms deliver milk in my street yet only one firm delivers newspapers. The former arrangement is seemingly less efficient because two vehicles and two milkmen doing the job implies some wasteful duplication. However, it does lead to competition, and neither milkman levies a delivery charge (at least explicitly) whereas the newsagent does.

It would be tempting and comforting to say that the invisible hand of the market mechanism oversees such operations. That is, the optimal number of milkmen is two and of newsagents one. But why should that be? The standard theorems of welfare economics assume away fixed costs (increasing returns) of the sort that both milkman and newsagent incur — each additional customer costing less to supply than average cost, at least within a certain range.

There are therefore two questions of importance to us, and we will stay with the milk/newspapers example. First, given there is a monopoly on newspapers, is intervention required? The monopolist is normally considered to exploit consumers by charging a high price and thereby destroying some consumer surplus. *If* the monopolist's position is naturally precarious, that is if there are many potential entrepreneurs looking to supply papers, then its pricing behaviour may well be tempered, so governmental intervention need not be required. If, on the other hand, the position is well-established, monopoly power may be considerable, leading to high prices. In this case, if intervention were available at zero cost, it would be desirable.

Secondly, is the position on milk optimal? If there is wasteful duplication, governmental (or neighbourhood) intervention is in principle desirable to award the street's milk contract to one firm, then if necessary to control its pricing behaviour. Alternatively, why have private supply of milk? Since the industry is in any case organized in some particulars by the Milk Marketing Board, a governmental agency, why not award them the contract for nationwide milk supply?

These are the topics that will occupy discussion in the next chapter and, to some extent, in later ones also. Using the milk/newspapers context has made them seen trivial: few people would find sensible the idea of a state monolith in milk supply or rigorous persecution of small-time dealers in newspapers by some all-seeing agency. This serves as a very useful warning. In the context of giant industries such as electricity supply the questions take on considerable significance. Consequently, substantial efforts to intervene (or to decide whether and in what way to intervene) are desirable in principle. In cases like newspaper delivery, they are most probably undesirable, except perhaps along the lines of occasional forays by bodies such as the Monopolies Commission.

Returning to the three possibilities, consider the second, where competition exists and produces tolerably efficient results, but these are deemed undesirable. For example, competition may dictate that supplying letter delivery service to, and maintaining 'phone boxes in, remote areas, is inefficient. Competition in bus services may mean heavy traffic on well-used routes and no service on others. Such situations may or may not be efficient, but the goal of equity may also be important.

Economists tend to shy away from equity as a goal, in the belief that if transfers are desirable they should be made on a lump sum or income taxation basis rather than being piecemeal on particular goods. Since none of these activities is costless, however, the situation is not quite as clear as suggested by economists who propose that efficiency should be the only goal. Transaction costs can be important.

To take an example, suppose it is considered generally socially desirable (on the basis, say, of needs; Weitzman, 1977) that everyone has the chance of access to a reasonable water supply. This could be done by charging on the basis of marginal supply cost for water (if feasible) and redistributing income, to allow people to allocate their income between water and other goods on the basis of market prices, or charging on a basis more related to income than to use (e.g. based upon property valuations). The latter is less efficient in producing a water supply, leading to more consumption than otherwise, but it may be a relatively efficient way of ensuring an equal chance of access to it.

Perhaps such arguments are beside the main point, which is to cover the natural monopoly case. However, it is important to appreciate that any particular case of regulation seldom arises with just a single aim. We are separating out one aspect for analysis, but doing this is slightly artificial.

At this stage we should look briefly at the third and final possibility, and with it some cases we shall not be discussing in this book. One long-established form of regulation, which has a well-established pedigree in the economics literature, is correction for externalities which break the link between competition and efficiency. Many industrial activities impose external effects, usually detrimental ones, on the wider community. To take an example of some current interest, power stations fired by fossil fuels emit wastes which later, it seems, create acid rain. Accordingly, the marginal social cost of production is greater than the marginal (private) cost to the firm. Nuclear powered stations also arguably create negative externalities, of course. A third illustration is asbestos manufacture, which is implicated in fatal illness amongst employees and others.

Undoubtedly, left to themselves some manufacturers would feel bound to institute corrective measures in the processes, or pay compensation, but many would not. If, say, the acid rain falls in another country, the pressure upon a particular producer may be weak. Hence the long history of Factory Acts, the Alkali Inspectorate and so on, a history of regulation to correct detrimental externalities by direct or indirect means.[1]

Externalities could exist even with perfectly informed consumers of the final product. Economic Man, seeing two boxes of chocolates, of which one is cheaper because the manufacturer has not had to pay for consequential damage to some third party, would choose that cheaper box.

Similarly with public goods: there may be many potential suppliers of television broadcasts, but funding them presents a problem. If it is easy for Economic Man to receive the broadcast without paying, then he will not pay. The better he appraises the situation, the less likely he is to pay. If everyone thinks like that, the broadcast is not supplied and everyone is worse off. Hence the recourse to licensing (i.e. regulation) or indirect means of payment (advertising).

When consumers are not perfectly informed, additional problems arise. If you were to fly to Athens for the first time and take a taxi to an address in the city, you would be unable to assess whether the route was circuitous, or the baggage charge was normal. If the owner of the insurance company covering your house contents had absconded to Fiji, you might not discover this until your house was burgled and the company would not answer the telephone. Hence there is another reason for regulation, to protect consumers who cannot be the best judges of their own welfare in all regards.

Of course some cases of self-regulation would be profitable because they increase trade (an example might be the association of life insurance offices), but others might be socially desirable yet bedevilled by public good problems — who is to fund the regulatory body? In many areas, the state has stepped in to perform such acts. Examples abound in the professions, for example the question of auditors and joint stock companies, or solicitors and conveyancing. The latter, incidentally, illustrates another point, that concerning 'capture theory' which will be raised and dealt with at greater length later in the chapter (see p. 7).

---

[1]Here we may note that there are alternatives to regulation, particularly private court actions, but they may (or may not) be less efficient.

Finally, we should note an important qualification. Regulation is often a political issue. In fact, politics may have more to say about the actual extent of a regulatory framework than does economics. Politicians take up views, and react to industries' actions. Special interests can triumph. Moreover, those acting for the politicians similarly have a capacity to play an active role. Some of these issues should be addressed, even though the book is essentially about economics. In fact, I shall adopt a compromise; the next section will examine theories concerning why regulation occurs, but in the way economists have analysed this phenomenon.

1.3 Positive theories of regulation

Essentially, formulating a theory of regulation involves imputing motives to the various bodies involved in regulation; various theories are obtained by imputing various motives. Leaving aside the firms (whose actions will be discussed in more detail in chapters 4 and 5), we still have to consider the politicians and the regulatory agencies. Some theories concern themselves more with the motives of one than the other — seldom is the whole chain of actions discussed. Therefore sometimes one reads into the theory more than might be there.

A very common (but perhaps naive) view on regulation is the *public interest* theory. Here the government responds to market imperfections in proportions according with the extent of imperfection. Thus, industries which only occasionally are problematic would not be subject to continual regulation but rather would be liable to lightning attacks by the Monopolies Commission or whatever. Industries which, because of the extent of their natural monopolies and their size, impinged very extensively on everyday life would be controlled more directly. Thus alleged market failures in the area of advertisement hoardings would be a topic for the Monopolies Commission, whereas water supply might be expected to involve a regulatory authority or public supply agency. In the public interest view also, regulators perform their allotted tasks as a sacred trust. This, presumably one could say, maximizes their utility.

From the societal point of view, the public interest theory presents an ideal. The only question left is the extent to which corrective measures should be carried out, and this can (in principle!) be solved by equating marginal benefits with marginal costs. Most people would agree though that there is evidence clearly inconsistent with some aspects of the public interest view.

One facet of a critique would be that there are areas that do not fit the category of natural monopolies, and yet are subject to extensive regulation of the type under discussion. The obvious example is agriculture, usually employed as an illustration in chapters on perfect competition in introductory texts. Yet agricultural markets are extensively distorted by governmental agencies setting quotas, purchasing at agreed prices, subsidizing certain categories of production and so on. In the UK it is commonly agreed that this happens at least in part because of the extent to which farming, relative to industrial, interests are 'understood' in most Conservative cabinets (and even some Labour ones!).

The other side to the critique, again a common one in the UK, is that public agencies by no means serve the public interest alone but instead indulge in many other activities which appear to benefit the regulators' interests rather more. Certain daily newspapers delight in exposing wasteful practices in governmental departments, quasi-governmental agencies and so on.

Of course, both of these are rather unfocused attacks. We should inquire whether there are other theories capable of giving better explanations before abandoning the one we have. Two theories, at least, have some claim to do this. One is the *capture theory*, which relates to the critique of agencies once set up. Whatever the original guidelines given them, goes the argument, the agents get drawn into doing what is in the best interest of those they are regulating − they are, wittingly or unwittingly, captured by the people they are supposed to be policing (see, for example, Stigler, 1971).

Again, examples can be produced in favour of, and against, this hypothesis. There would be some truth in the assertion that traffic commissioners have the welfare of 'bus operators very much at heart when fixing fares; similar things could be said of airline regulators. On the other hand, what if, to take Posner's example (1974), an agency is called upon to regulate two opposing groups, like the Interstate Communications Commission who deal with truckers, railroads and bargees? Moreover, it is very difficult to explain moves like the phasing out of the United States Civil Aeronautics Board (discussed in chapter 7) in terms of this theory.

Arguably more powerful, since it is more general, is the *Economic theory of regulation*. This has as its main thrust the idea that regulation itself is subject to economic laws. The government is in a position to supply regulation and, indeed, it might commonly be eager to do so, if ministers gain utility in proportion to the size of resources they control. Certain industries will demand regulation if it helps to improve the position of the firms within them. Thus farmers may perceive benefits in bodies such as the Milk Marketing Board through gains in selling power, although other aspects of the Board's operations may be undesirable to them. These benefits depend upon the difference between returns under regulation and those without it, hence, as Posner (1974) suggests, on the gains from cartelization and the ease of forming cartels. Interest groups that are large and diffuse will tend to be dominated by small, tightly knit groups that have a lot to gain (Peltzman, 1976); thus these will often, though not inevitably, be the producers (for a counter-example see Wenders, 1986). In sum, special interests of politically effective groups rather than socially desirable interests triumph.

As has been said, some observations would appear consistent with this viewpoint. Much more equivocal is whether the theory has any predictive content. Just because an industry desires a convenient method of cartel formation, that does not mean it will necessarily get it. As an example from a slightly different sphere, the Lancashire cotton spinners were forced to abandon an agreement on pricing (In Yarn Spinners' Agreement LR1 RP, pp. 118–99), despite pleading the threat to employment. In fact, Posner (1974) points out that there is very little research indeed that can be considered as a direct test of the economic theory, and the results of these few tests are not clear cut. Thus there seems nothing inevitable about the process. What is more, such actions as imposing regulation, though they may tend to acquire a momentum of their own, are nevertheless hardly irreversible. Preferences can change, and if different political parties have differing views, a private rather than social interest cannot be expected to persist for ever.

There is another strand to the Economic theory of regulation, which is that once the agency has an objective, those charged with carrying out the policies do so to the best of their ability. This is not because they wish to act in the public interest as exemplified in the values of their political masters, but rather because they wish to succeed in their careers and the way to do so is to appear efficient. This is a rather strict version of the managerial labour market theory (Fama, 1980) which will be discussed in chapter 3. Yet, again, it is surely difficult to test.

Also, evidence suggesting that regulation in fact has no effect goes against this viewpoint. Critics of regulation from the standpoint of economic theory cannot have it both ways. Assuming that regulation has the potential to promote social benefits, either it is effective, but in the wrong directions, or it is ineffective; it can scarcely be both. We also have the paradox that (as Posner, 1972, p.153 admits) those same people who tend to argue that the common law promotes efficiency also reject the idea that regulatory law does the same thing.

One more positive criticism of the Economic theory of regulation is that it lacks sufficient structure to make it testable. Because 'utility maximizing' objectives can be imputed to government or regulators, almost anything can fit with it. The bones of the policy-makers and their agents must be fleshed out in order to refine the theory.

To take the policy-makers first, what do they maximize? One plausible self-interest goal is re-election. Therefore, in this variant, the politician will indulge in promoting regulatory activities that tend to do this; the MP of a farming constituency promotes tighter regulations on imported meat and so on. This provides the framework for a theory of why some areas are regulated and some not, albeit a partial one since it depends on the pattern of interests. This does not really explain how the regulation will be conducted, as this is more a feature of the regulators than of the politicians, if there is any slack in the relationship between government and regulatory agents.

If the regulators have discretion, what will they do? In general, it seems sensible to suggest that any discretion will be exercised so as to improve regulators' utility (along the lines of what would be expected from a managerial utility maximization model like Williamson's, 1963). Thus aspects such as status, security and so on are likely to be important. This, however, is still not particularly operational as a theory.

One way to move in that direction by identifying different underlying structures is suggested by de Alessi (1974). He points out that there are two general types of regulatory bodies – independent agencies and government bureaux – and that performance is likely to differ between them. Commissioners normally have fixed-term posts at given salaries whilst civil servants move from post to post. Hence commissioners are likely to try to minimize conflict, in order to improve their chances of remaining in office, and they are likely to go for 'quiet life' options to gain non-pecuniary income. Civil servants, in contrast, are likely to seek active regulation in order to increase perceived responsibilities and hence, according to de Alessi, improve their chances of upgrading the post. He claims some empirical support for these predictions.

The foregoing survey does not claim to be complete; in fact only a small sample from the wide range of contributions has been considered. Enough has been said, however, to make it clear that regulation need not necessarily act in the public interest. Where do we go from here?

Undoubtedly regulation of industry has the potential power to improve social welfare and to say we should abandon it because it may not always do so is nihilistic. In the same way, criticisms of the Monopolies Commission on the grounds that perceived monopoly welfare losses are low are misplaced; what matters is what would transpire in the Commission's absence. Few people would argue that national defence should be abandoned in favour of private armies because defence chiefs presently make decisions having regard to inter-service rivalry, relationships with defence manufacturers, and so on, rather than making socially ideal decisions.

So, what positive lessons do we glean from a consideration of the theory?

First, that since regulatory actions are normally costly, *de minimis* provisions should apply. It does not make sense to regulate the newsagent in the example used in section 1.2. Secondly, agency discretion should be limited in so far as this is compatible with efficient operational decisions. Thirdly, ideas as well as interests are important influences on policy. Governments may wish, purely for political reasons, to control various industries (or not to do so). One of the traditional planks of Labour Party policy in the UK has been to own the 'commanding heights' of the economy, though it is never completely clear what these include. Similarly, French and Italian governments have sought to take some equity stake in certain industries. Things can go both ways, of course. The present UK Conservative government seems eager to remove controls even in cases where many people consider them beneficial, for equally political reasons; but it has done so far more quickly in some areas than others. We are equally in need of a positive theory of deregulation. Such actions may be perceived as regulation or deregulation and may have economic effects (as will be discussed in chapter 4 and elsewhere), but they may essentially be a response to special interests or to fashions in ideas.

We are essentially interested here in cases where important natural monopoly industries exist and the choice is between a free market and various forms of regulation. If regulation is involved, those charged with performing the surveillance should be seen as responsive to consumer as well as producer interests, if they are to reflect societies' preferences. But that requires that both sets of interests be represented effectively. The question is, what sorts of models and control frameworks are best at getting round the various problems that will be encountered in designing regulatory schemes?

1.4   An example

In order to provide an impetus for the study, and also an introduction to the analysis of chapter 2, consider the following *very much simplified* illustration. Assume the UK gas industry is setting monopoly prices. The demand for gas is approximated by a linear curve, along the lines of D in figure 1.1. Corresponding to this is the marginal revenue curve MR. Marginal costs are falling slightly, as illustrated by curve MC, so the industry is a natural monopoly.

At present, given these assumptions, output is y_m and price is p_m. If output could be expanded up to the point y_s where price equals marginal cost, there would be an extensive gain in social welfare, namely the shaded

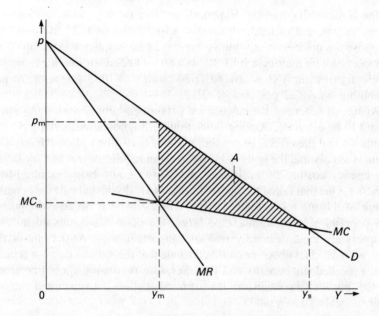

Figure 1.1 Monopoly welfare loss

area.[2] Making the simplifying assumptions that there are no income effects and that any effects on the distribution of income are unimportant, this area may stand for the true change in social welfare. So how large is it?

In theory, the calculation is straightforward. Following Schmalensee (1982) the area marked A may be written as the triangular area to which it approximates:

$$A = \tfrac{1}{2}(p_m - MC_m)(y_s - y_m)$$
$$= \tfrac{1}{2}L_m(p_m y_m)K$$

where L_m is the price-marginal cost margin, $p_m y_m$ is sales revenue at current prices and $K(=y_s - y_m/y_m)$ is a number somewhat in excess of one because marginal cost is falling. If marginal cost were constant, K would be one and the formula would be exact.

To get an approximate feel for the size of the loss, in 1985 according

[2]The additional revenue plus consumer surplus is given by the area under the demand curve between y_m and y_s; the additional cost by the area under the marginal cost curve between y_m and y_s.

to the National Income and Expenditure 'Blue Book', £4046 million was spent on gas, out of total consumers' expenditure of £213,208 million. Suppose the price–cost margin is one-third (this implies a mark-up of 50 per cent, which may be a bit high, but let us underestimate K, at unity). These figures imply A is around £670 million at 1985 prices or, to put it another way, 0.2 per cent of GDP.

Again, to reiterate, the calculation performed here is not in any sense meant to be accurate. Among other things, it ignores industrial gas consumption and the effects of regulation other than direct price effects. The point is simply that the potential benefits from regulation can be very large. An agency costing £6 million a year to run could bring hundred-fold benefits. One that failed to capture or otherwise dissipated half the benefits would still bring social returns over 50 times its cost. Because the potential benefits of regulation are so large, the questions discussed in later chapters are most decidedly real and important ones. At the end of the day, an individual observer could conclude that the various costs of regulation exceeded the benefits and that therefore regulation should be abandoned, but such a conclusion, if warranted at all, is not warranted without a great deal of analysis.

A guide to the literature

There have been a great many studies of market failures which provide an a priori case for intervention – welfare economics texts such as Boadway and Bruce (1984) or summary chapters in books such as Varian (1978) will serve. Stigler (1975, chapter 7) offers a provocative treatment. The particular case of natural monopoly will be developed further in chapter 2. As far as the public interest theory of regulation is concerned, this is largely an implicit rather than explicit model. The Economic theory in its various forms has been extensively discussed and developed. Stigler's paper (1975, chapter 8) is influential, and in particular Posner's paper (1974) is an important discussion of the model. Useful commentaries are provided by Wilson (1980) (on political aspects) and by Tomlinson (1983). Mitnick (1980) has an extensive analysis of the various theories, together with many other matters that will be discussed later on. For a more practical assessment, see Hilton (1972). Joskow and Noll (1983) provide a good general survey of the economics of regulation.

2

Regulation and Natural Monopoly

The previous chapter made the point that economic regulation involves controls on pricing and controls on entry. This chapter examines the theoretical justification for such controls, that is, the case for intervention.

In a perfectly competitive industry, the market solves two connected problems. First it solves the problem of the efficient industry cost structure − the allocation of production within the industry in such a way that the desired output is produced at minimum cost. Output is allocated among plants so that all are producing at the lowest point on their average cost curves. Secondly, it solves the problem of the efficient pricing structure. Consumers pay prices equal to marginal costs and this brings forth exactly enough output from the industry in the sense that it makes just sufficient firms viable.

Unfortunately from this point of view not all industries are perfectly competitive. Hence in such cases we cannot expect the twin goals to be met; in fact it may be that some compromise position has to be reached. It would appear, on the face of it, that this problem of satisfying the two goals is least likely to be achieved in a monopoly situation. The compromise, in this case, may therefore imply some outside regulation. This chapter examines these questions from a theoretical standpoint within the framework of natural monopoly industries. Much of what is said would be true also (in a modified form) for small-number natural oligopolies, but I shall not examine such questions here.

Let us start with a simple and rather stark model along the lines of Peacock and Rowley (1972). There is a specific product which has falling average costs throughout the relevant output range as given by demand. Hence production by a monopolist is cheapest. Also, a competitive equilibrium cannot exist because at the point where price equals each firm's marginal cost, profits would increase with increasing output so each firm would wish to increase output and thereby achieve lower costs. Since they all do this, they all make losses. Monopoly equilibrium is possible. Specifically a monopolist in residence will equate marginal revenue and marginal cost and earn substantial profits as a result, yet (small scale) entry would be barred because costs of producing low outputs are so high. The situation is depicted in figure 2.1, with the monopolist's price and output given by (p_m, y_m).

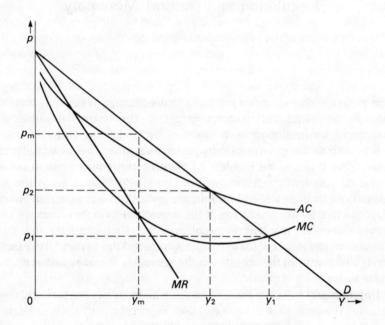

Figure 2.1 Natural monopoly and regulation

The monopoly outcome is not socially Pareto-optimal. At least three potentially Pareto-superior situations may be identified. First, and optimally, price could be set equal to marginal costs. In that case, denoted (p_1, y_1), losses would be made (unless it was only the marginal consumer who was paying marginal costs with others being charged differentially higher prices according to their willingness to pay − on which, see below and chapter 4). Hence, lump sum transfers would be required to ensure breakeven, in which case public control seems a sensible solution, with the necessary funds coming from general taxation.

Alternatively, the industry could be in the hands of a private firm which would have its prices regulated by the state in such a way as to earn what approximates to a normal rate of return on capital employed. The solution here would be (p_2, y_2), assuming efficient regulation (and making some abstractions).

A third alternative, proposed by Demsetz (1968), is for the rights to supply to be auctioned off to bidders whose bids would be in the form of a contract to supply at a given price (rather like bids for the construction of a motorway). Given sufficient bidders, price may be expected to approximate average cost, and output would be y_2.

All these solutions are the subject of further analysis in later chapters. But before we move on to institutional questions, we should recognize that whilst figure 2.1 illustrates a natural monopoly, it by no means exhausts the possibilities. Nor, it transpires, is it clearly the case that any controls are needed. The model must be extended. This is done first by examining the analytics of the cost and demand sides, the subject of this chapter, and then concentrating more on the internal structure of the firm (in chapter 3), in order to move on to the question of efficiency.

Our path here is as follows. First we will examine what a natural monopoly actually is. Thus section 2.1 will discuss single-product natural monopoly. Because this does not give sufficient insights, the analysis is extended to multiproduct natural monopoly in section 2.2, which necessitates first going into multiproduct cost and pricing concepts. Then we will examine its *effects*. Section 2.3 covers the key ideas of contestability and sustainability (roughly, ease of entry and natural protection from inefficient entry) and section 2.4 draws the various concepts together to consider the case for regulation. The situation is summarized in section 2.5.

2.1 Single-product natural monopoly

To start with, we must address the question of the definition of 'natural monopoly'. In the earlier example, the average cost curve fell continuously and there was a monopolist in residence in the industry. Perhaps surprisingly, neither of these is necessary for an industry to be a natural monopoly at some output levels, though the average cost curve must certainly have a falling portion.

The first point to make is that the term 'natural monopoly' could bear two interpretations. One is that there would only ever be one firm in the industry. But, on reflection, this depends for example on one's theory of oligopoly. If we take Cournot's time-honoured example of the mineral water duopoly, with the exception that we suppose developing a spring involves a fixed cost F, after which all the water desired can be extracted at a constant marginal cost (of c, possibly zero), then we have a natural monopoly in the sense that average cost is continually declining. However, if two firms can each make profits producing at the Cournot output levels, this will be a non-cooperative duopoly equilibrium in outputs. Yet if instead of choosing outputs, the firms indulge in price-setting behaviour (on which see below), any equilibrium is likely to involve only one firm. Supposing in a Bertrand-type model that the industry has reached the point at which both firms are breaking even, there will still be a tendency to cut the price to drive the other firm out of business until the price reaches the level at which the victorious monopolist is breaking even. The alternative interpretation, now generally accepted, is that it is more efficient if there is only one firm. As Baumol et al. (1977) put it, 'By a *natural monopoly* we mean an industry whose cost function is such that no combination of several firms can produce an industry output vector as cheaply as it can be provided by a single supplier' (p. 350). So, figure 2.1 shows a situation which is sufficient for there to be a natural monopoly, but it is not in fact necessary.

Costs can be rising in a natural monopoly industry. This is because the key (necessary and sufficient) concept for natural monopoly is (strict) *subadditivity*. The cost function must satisfy the condition that:

$$C(Y) < \sum_i C(y_i); \; \Sigma y_i = Y; \; i = 1, 2, 3, \ldots, k; \; k \geq 2;$$

no combination of two or more firms can produce the desired output Y at a lesser cost than one firm by splitting that output in any way between themselves.

To illustrate, suppose we consider an industry where any firm is able to operate on the U-shaped average cost curve $C(y_i) = a + by_i^2$ and where there may be either one or two firms. *If* two firms are involved, they must be used in such a way that industry costs are minimized. Industry costs are:

$$\begin{aligned} C[Y(2)] &= C(x) + C(Y - x) \\ &= 2a + bx^2 + b(Y - x)^2 = 2a + 2bx^2 + bY^2 - 2bYx. \end{aligned}$$

Thus, to split output optimally:

$$\frac{\partial C[Y(2)]}{\partial x} = 4bx - 2bY = 0$$

i.e. $\quad x = Y/2.$

Therefore, to minimize industry costs with two firms, and with this cost structure, they must each produce half.[1]

---

[1]In general, determining the split between firms is not straightforward (see Baumol et al., 1982, ch. 5, app. 2).

We may now compare the costs of two firms producing with the costs of one. One is cheaper than two when:

$$C[Y(1)] < C[Y(2)] = 2C[Y(1)/2].$$

Substituting for the functional form yields:

$$a + bY^2 < 2\left[a + b\left(\frac{Y}{2}\right)^2\right]$$

or

$$Y < \sqrt{2a/b}.$$

This may be compared with the minimum point of the average cost curve:

$$\frac{C(y_i)}{y_i} = \sqrt{a/b}$$

Hence we have the industry cost arrangement depicted in figure 2.2.

It is clear that when demand is at level D_1, the industry is a natural monopoly, and when demand is at level D_2, as we have just discovered,

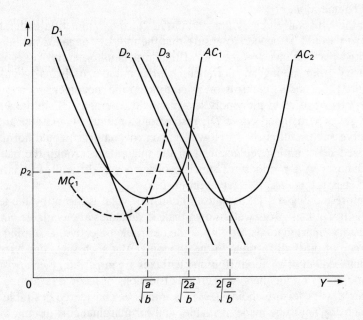

Figure 2.2 U-shaped costs, natural monopoly, and demand

the industry is still a natural monopoly. If demand is at level D_3, the industry becomes a natural duopoly (and it will not cease being so until well after $2\sqrt{(a/b)}$ units of output are demanded).

The purpose of these calculations has been to demonstrate that rising average cost is consistent with natural monopoly. They also illustrate three other points of importance. First, as a general point, an industry may change from being a natural monopoly not only through changes in underlying technology but also through changes in demand. In particular, if demand is growing, an industry may move away from natural monopoly status. Secondly, marginal cost pricing in natural monopoly does not necessarily require a subsidy. With demand curve D_2 a natural monopolist charging marginal cost (MC_1) would better than break even.

However, thirdly, a natural monopolist may be vulnerable to entry even when charging average cost and being perfectly efficient. Such entry must, perforce, be inefficient, because of the subadditivity-based definition of natural monopoly. How, then, can it occur? The answer is that it must be partial entry, a firm offering to supply *part of the market only* at a price less than p_2. People offered such a contract are likely to take it, but in supplying it, a firm destroys the ideal industry structure and the market of the incumbent firm. A natural monopoly in such a position is said to be not *sustainable*. Obviously, it is better for society to avoid such destructive competition.

In the situation given by demand curve D_2, the implication is that two controls would be needed to ensure that the industry engaged in socially optimal performance (see below). First, restraints on entry to keep the industry from having an inefficiently large number of firms would be required. Secondly, controls on price to keep the incumbent monopolist from raising price to monopoly levels should be employed. In the situation given by demand curve D_1, restrictions on entry would appear not to serve any useful purpose. However, controls on price would normally be needed, assuming replacement of the incumbent through the market mechanism by a producer of superior efficiency is difficult, that is, the market is not *contestable* (see section 2.3).

Before moving on, let us pause to consider what is meant by the term 'socially optimal'. It is well known that, if subsidies are available where necessary, marginal cost pricing is the desirable objective, assuming the absence of other distortions in the economy. But such subsidies have to be financed out of taxation. If lump sum taxes are infeasible, then any such taxation (e.g. on incomes) will create distortions of its own (affecting for example work/leisure choices). Hence it may be considered desirable for the subsidy not to be made available, and for marginal cost pricing to be replaced by average cost pricing. Within our example, there is only one way to practise average cost pricing, but this is not generally so within multiproduct frameworks. In order to gain further insights, we must extend the model in this direction.

2.2 Multiproduct costs, pricing and subadditivity

Extending the analysis to multiproduct firms creates two difficulties. First, we shall have to inquire into what is meant by a multiproduct natural monopoly, in particular into the cost conditions that are associated with it. Further precision is required, for example, in discussing what is meant by economies of scale and the relationship of these to natural monopoly. Second, a multiproduct firm required to break even has degrees of freedom in its pricing which are unavailable to a single-product firm. Setting prices on average equal to marginal cost can be done in more than one way, and some will be socially superior to others. Both these analyses are developed below.

Cost concepts

My main illustrations of cost relationships will use two outputs only, and we will not be concerned with factor input requirements. An analogy may then usefully be drawn between the one input-two output production function and the rather more familiar two input-one output function. In that case, there are three dimensions to consider, but often partial relationships are examined. For example, one can examine returns to scale by taking a ray from the origin. In this context, returns to scale may be measured as S = average cost/marginal cost with $S > 1$ implying economies of scale. But also of importance are returns to a factor, keeping the other constant.

In a similar way we can first examine ray average costs and returns to scale along a ray. Define ray average costs as:

$$RAC(Y) = \frac{C(tY_o)}{t}$$

where Y_o is a unit bundle of a particular mix of output (e.g. $3y_1 + 2y_2$) and t is the number of units in the bundle (so that when $t = 3$, $C(tY_o) = C(9y_1 + 6y_2)$). Fairly obviously, declining ray average costs occur when multiplying all outputs by t less than multiplies costs by t, so that *RAC* falls as t increases. This links with *a* definition of multiproduct scale economies:

$$S = \frac{C(Y)}{\Sigma y_i MC_i} \tag{2.1}$$

where y_i are output dimensions and Y is the vector of outputs, MC_i being the partial marginal costs of each output. Thus it relates total costs (in the numerator) to attributable costs (in the denominator). If RAC is falling, output-weighted marginal costs are below total cost so $S > 1$, and vice versa.

We can also examine the behaviour of the cost surface as we vary only one of the outputs, the analogy here being returns to a factor. Define average incremental costs of output 1 as:

$$AIC_1(Y) = \frac{C(y_1, y_2) - C(0, y_2)}{y_1}$$

This gives rise to a natural measure of product-specific returns to scale as:

$$S_i = \frac{AIC_i(Y)}{MC_i}$$

where $MC_i = \partial C(Y)/\partial y_i$. Again $S_i > 1$ implies these are (product-specific) economies of scale.

There is another concept of importance for multiproduct firms, which is different from what has gone before. This is the idea of economies of scope. If:

$$C(y_1, y_2) < C(y_1, 0) + C(0, y_2)$$

then there are said to be economies of scope at the output level concerned. One way to think of this is as a type of economies of joint production.

To take an example: a car manufacturer may notice that the average cost of producing a model falls as greater numbers of the model are produced. All other things equal, it looks as if producing more of the model is beneficial. However, producing this model alongside another may give rise to benefits — perhaps they have common components, or common design and marketing costs, in which case there are shareable inputs. Take the component case: suppose both cars use the same gearbox, purchased from an outside source. It is necessary to keep a small stock of gearboxes because there is some uncertainty about how many will be used on any day, and reordering subjects the firm to some delay. The firm that produces both models need not keep twice as many gearboxes in store to have the same availability as would two firms each producing one model because, unless the uncertainties are perfectly correlated, it is less likely that high production of both models will be required on any particular day than that high production of either one will.

Two other, rather briefer, examples will illustrate the relevance to potential natural monopoly industries. Economies of scope are likely to arise in (i) railways, between passenger and freight transport using the same lines and (ii) electricity generation, between peak and off-peak periods, some of the same equipment being used.

Economies of scope do not necessarily mean that producing both models (or whatever) is better for the firm than producing one, because all other things may not be equal. Specifically, the products may be gross substitutes in demand: increased sales of one will detract from sales of the other. Therefore, producing the package rather than one product means the firm gains the economies of scope but loses some economies of scale in the product that it would have produced more intensively.

Partly because of this problem, it is useful to define a more general concept, transray convexity, which involves considering bundles of two (for simplicity) goods consisting of different proportions. Let bundle $Y^* = (y_1^*, y_2^*)$ and $Y^{**} = (y_1^{**}, y_2^{**})$. Then a cost function is transray convex if:

$$C(\lambda Y^* + (1 - \lambda) Y^{**}) < \lambda C(Y^*) + (1 - \lambda) C(Y^{**}).$$

To see the relationship between the two concepts, consider the special case where $Y^* = (y_1, 0)$, $Y^{**} = (0, y_2)$. We than have:

$$C(\lambda y_1 + (1 - \lambda) y_2) < \lambda C(y_1, 0) + (1 - \lambda) C(0, y_2).$$

The left hand side of this expression involves outputs of each product smaller, respectively, than y_1 and y_2. Hence the meaning of the expression as a whole is that, as far as costs are concerned, economies of scope are sufficient to counteract the loss in economies of scale in each product line.

Diagrammatically, the relationships between the concepts are illustrated in figure 2.3. Transray convexity involves looking at cost behaviour in the vertical plane along (say) the line AB. Economies of scope involve comparing costs at point C with those at A and B, whereas multiproduct economies of scale examine behaviour along OC, and product-specific economies of scale are concerned with costs as we move along AC or BC.

There are two main uses to which we will put these concepts. First, they are related to subadditivity — the question of whether or not the industry is a natural monopoly. Secondly, they relate to sustainability — can the ideal structure, in this case a monopoly, be maintained by the established firm, or will it be vulnerable to entry?

Pricing behaviour

If scale economies are extensive, marginal cost pricing of each of two (say) dimensions of output would lead to substantial shortfalls. This is easily

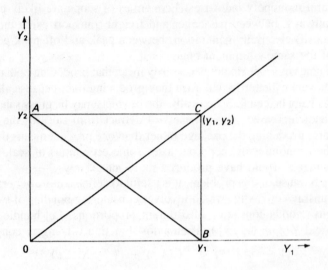

Figure 2.3   Relationships between cost concepts

seen: in $S = C(Y)/\Sigma y_i MC_i$, output-weighted marginal costs are the denominator and total costs the numerator, so when $S > 1$ prices fail to cover costs. Therefore, if the firms involved are to break even, how should they do it? There are at least three important possibilities: cost-based pricing, valued-based pricing and price discrimination.

Cost-based pricing is fairly straightforward. The price marginal cost margin on each product is set equal to $(1 - 1/S)$ where S is the degree of scale economies appropriate to the total output mix. The firm then just breaks even. To see this, observe that the suggested formula is:

$$\frac{p_i - MC_i}{p_i} = 1 - \frac{1}{S}.$$

Hence

$$p_i y_i - MC_i y_i = \left(1 - \frac{1}{S}\right) p_i y_i$$

or

$$MC_i y_i = \frac{1}{S} p_i y_i.$$

Aggregating over all products and comparing with the definition of S, we find $\Sigma\, p_i y_i = C(Y)$ — revenues are just sufficient to cover costs.

In the single-product firm context, there are in theory solutions to the problem of marginal cost pricing being insufficient to yield a profit. Specifically, the firm might charge different consumers different prices. As a polar case, Lindahl pricing involves each customer paying according to his/her marginal benefit from the good. Then, if production of the good is socially worthwhile, the revenues will exceed the cost of production. However, as a practical scheme this is infeasible, since consumers have no direct incentive to reveal their benefit schedules, nor can they easily be encouraged to do so (Green and Laffont, 1979). Nevertheless, there are often possibilities for the supplier to charge different people different amounts for the same good based approximately upon marginal value, for example a fixed charge plus an amount dependent upon intensity of use. Such *nonlinear outlay schedules* (sometimes, confusingly, called nonlinear pricing) are discussed in chapter 4. Given the way the literature has developed, we shall spend more time here on the idea of *value*-based pricing — charging prices in proportion to value of the service to the user on a multiproduct basis.[2]

Value-based pricing involves margins being different on different products, but fixed on each individual product. It is often called *Ramsey pricing*, after Frank Ramsey who first framed this (or, rather, a similar) problem in 1928. The problem can be thought of as maximizing consumer surplus (here total surplus minus resource costs) arising from the set of products, subject to the breakeven constraint, i.e. choose y_1 to y_n to maximize:

$$CS \equiv \sum_{i=1}^{n} \left[\int_0^{y_i} p_i(x) \cdot dx - C(Y) \right] \tag{2.2}$$

subject to $\Pi \equiv R(Y) - C(Y) = 0$ where $R(Y)$ is the revenue accruing from sales of all the products and x is a variable of integration. The single-product equivalent, which has a trivial solution — set price equal to average cost — is illustrated in figure 2.4.

Ramsey's problem may be solved by straightforward application of the Lagrangean multiplier technique. Using λ for the multiplier, the Lagrangean function is:

$$L = CS + \lambda\Pi$$

so that λ can be thought of as the weight (>0) attaching to the firm's profits

---

[2] Of course, the distinction between the two methods of discrimination is not as sharp as it may seem, since it is not clear what constitutes a product.

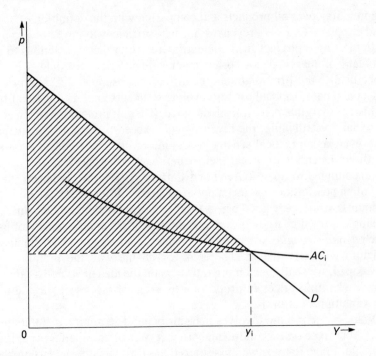

Figure 2.4   Ramsey pricing with one product

as opposed to consumer utility. The weight could be imposed exogenously, but here it is determined endogenously. From (2.2) the first order conditions yield:

$$p_i - \frac{\partial C}{\partial y_i} = - \lambda \left[\frac{\partial R}{\partial y_i} - \frac{\partial C}{\partial y_i} \right] \qquad (2.3)$$

The interpretation of marginal cost, $\partial C/\partial y_i$, has already been covered, but it is worth pointing out that the interpretation of marginal revenue, $\partial R/\partial y_i$, also needs some care. Assuming that product i has demand-side links with other products in the set, it will involve effects both on this product and on others. Thus, supposing this product is a substitute for the others, an increase in its output will shift the demand curves for the other products inward. On the other hand, if there are no relationships on the demand side, equation (2.3) can be simplified, because we can write marginal revenue as $p_i(1 - 1/\eta_i)$ where η_i is the elasticity of demand for product i (defined as a positive number). Then by rearrangement of (2.3):

$$\frac{p_i - MC_i}{p_i} = \left(\frac{\lambda}{1 + \lambda}\right) \frac{1}{\eta_i}.$$

Hence, margins on goods in relatively elastic demand should be lower than those on relatively inelastic demand. Also, as the constraint binds increasingly more tightly, λ will rise and the margin will approximate $(1/\eta_i)$, which is what a discriminating monopolist faced with several submarkets would charge.

Obviously, there are other pricing schemes a firm could employ, but none would seem on the face of it to be as compelling as the ones we have discussed here. So, leaving aside nonlinear outlay schedules until chapter 4, how might a societal choice be made between value- and cost-based pricing? The first point is that Ramsey pricing has advantages both in terms of static efficiency and also arguably in terms of equity over cost-based pricing. However, these advantages are unlikely to be important if scale economies are only limited in extent, and cost-based pricing is certainly easier to adopt. The other major point, which we are not yet in a position to discuss, relates to the state of competition and potential competition in the industry. Two important factors interact, one suggesting Ramsey pricing is superior, the other suggesting the contrary.

Multiproduct subadditivity

In discussing the single-product case, we found that subadditivity at the relevant output, the necessary and sufficient condition for natural monopoly, was not related in any close way to features of the cost function. The most we can say is that if there are still economies of scale unexploited, the industry is a natural monopoly. Therefore it will come as no surprise that in the multiproduct case there is no neat way to characterize subadditivity in terms of other concepts. All we can do is to find sets of conditions which are, and sets which are not, sufficient. In doing this, the discussion will be purely at the intuitive level.

Because economies of scale are a sufficient (not necessary) condition for subadditivity in the single-product case, it might be thought they are sufficient also in the multiproduct case. They are, in a very restricted sense: decreasing ray average costs or increasing returns to scale imply *ray* subadditivity. They do not imply subadditivity in general. Effectively, this can happen because there might be diseconomies of scope, so that individual production is cheaper than multi-output production. However, just to confuse matters, economies of scale plus economies of scope do not imply subadditivity. The reason why this can happen is (to recall figure 2.3) that economies of scope involve a comparison between points on the axes of a cost function drawn in output space, with an interior point. Their presence does not necessarily (though it will often, for smooth functions) imply anything about comparisons between various interior points.

Now, two sets of sufficient conditions relating to cost concepts we have covered earlier can be outlined. First, decreasing average incremental costs of each product plus economies of scope is sufficient to imply subadditivity. This is fairly clear intuitively, since the first part implies subadditivity in each product line, whilst the second part means that it is cheaper to produce the set of products together. Second, declining ray average costs plus transray convexity along any hyperplane through the output point will guarantee subadditivity. Intuitively, this condition succeeds where the 'economies of scale plus economies of scope' one did not because the comparison is between relevant interior points. We have ray subadditivity plus the fact that costs increase as we move off the ray.

Since this second sufficient condition turns out to be of some importance, it might be useful to have an intuitive idea of what is involved. Looking at the behaviour of costs as we increase all outputs proportionately along the ray we have a picture like figure 2.5a. Taking a section (hyperplane) across the cost function, gives us a picture like 2.5b. Hence a cost surface which exhibited both these features everywhere would have a shoehorn-like shape, with the handle at the origin, as in figure 2.5c.

The upshot of this difficulty in finding simple conditions relating to subadditivity is that to establish empirically that an industry is a natural monopoly is by no means straightforward (though see, for example, Evans and Heckman, 1984).

2.3 Contestability and sustainability

Having completed the definitional stage of the theoretical investigation of natural monopoly, we turn now to two intertwined issues of control. Economic regulation consists of controls on prices and on entry. Controls on prices are argued to reduce the extent of monopoly abuse. Yet intuitively, the scope for such abuse would be reduced if entry were easy. Why then the controls on entry? The effects of allowing or inhibiting entry are examined in this section first by investigating the plausibility of completely free entry, then by seeing whether firms can adopt policies to guard against entry. These analyses are combined in section 2.4 to assess the theoretical case for intervention.

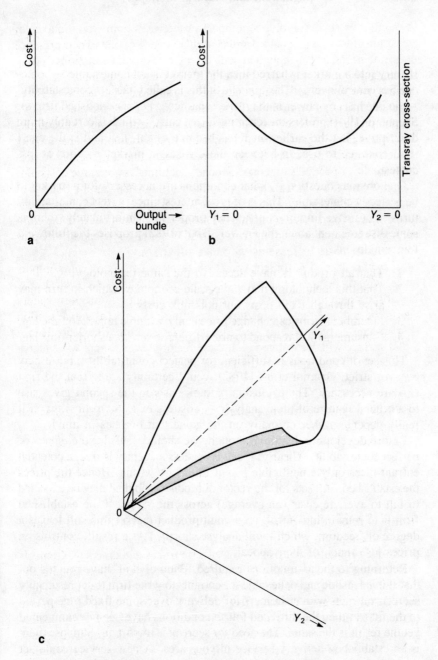

Figure 2.5 Declining ray average costs plus transray convexity

Contestability

If entry into a market is barred then the market is not contestable — someone has control over it. The opposite of this is called 'perfect contestability' — no one has any power in the market, particularly the established firm(s). Shepherd (1984) prefers the term 'ultra-free entry', which is certainly more descriptive, but the earlier term has become established and is the one I shall continue to use. In between these cases, a market is more or less contestable.

One obvious question is, what conditions are necessary for a market to be perfectly contestable? This is of great interest since perfect contestability turns out to have important efficiency properties. Unfortunately, there is some disagreement about the answer. Dixit (1982) proposes the following four conditions:

1 That all producers have access to the same technology.
2 That this technology may have scale economies which in turn may arise through fixed costs but not sunk costs.
3 Incumbent firms can change prices only within a non-zero time lag.
4 Consumers must respond to price differences with a shorter time lag.

This set of conditions is sufficient for perfect contestability, but it may be over-strict. Baumol et al. (1982) would certainly agree that the first two are necessary. The exclusion of sunk costs in the second gives rise to a crucial feature of their analysis — costless exit. As to the others, it really depends rather crucially on the game that one has in mind.

Before developing this point though, we should consider the *effects* of perfect contestability. Clearly, if exit is costless and entry is free, a potential entrant faces only a negligible loss if things go wrong. Hence the prices the established firm sets for the vector of products supplied may be expected to fall to average costs (on average) across the range, if the established firm is to remain in control. (In a multiproduct market this still leaves a degree of freedom, which I will analyse shortly.) As a result, controls on prices lose much of their appeal.

Returning to the assumptions required, Baumol et al. have pointed out that if it is feasible and believable for entrants to write firm (but presumably secret) contracts with customers for delivery over some fixed time period in the future, then the third and fourth conditions have been circumvented yet the result is the same. The need for secrecy is important. Suppose there is an established delivery service in your area. A new service could set up by gaining enough contracts with major customers of the old service to take over. People would only switch if the new price was below the old, but if the incumbent firm hears of these plans after (say) only one contract has been signed it may be able still to win the day by immediately offering all its other customers new terms.

If this will always happen, potential entrants will be deterred. Therefore we can probably conclude that conditions (3) and (4) or some close equivalent, are in fact necessary. Conditions (1) and (2) alone clearly are not enough and there can only be a limited number of ways of thinking of conditions which give the same results as (3) and (4).

The next obvious question concerns the reasonableness of such a range of conditions. Are they met in practice? The answer must be, seldom. In particular, there would appear to be at least one strategy by the incumbent which breaks the conditions as first laid out. This is the 'never knowingly undersold' strategy, by which the incumbent promises to reduce the price *ex post* should the consumer find that the good could have been obtained elsewhere more cheaply. Effectively, this means that the incumbent has to give no notice of price changes.

Turning to the consumer's view of these conditions, a customer who buys from a 'never knowingly undersold' (or, indeed, any) source presumably would benefit from occasionally looking elsewhere to police the claim (though there is a free-rider problem here — if the price reduction becomes general once any one consumer has complained, why not let someone else do it?). If a cheaper potential supplier is discovered, a firm contract between the parties may be signed. It is in both the firm's and the consumer's interests that this is for some extended period: in the case of the latter because search costs (presumably) are finite and so will not be worth incurring if there is only some probability of finding low prices, unless the benefits are substantial. The problem for the potential incumbent is that it has to get enough customers signed up to enable the prices quoted to be profitable. Hence there must be many people searching in the belief that lower prices will be found. However, this contradicts the point that it will not be optimal to search all the time. Therefore either the customers must continually be changing identity (so it is sensible for them to engage in some search) and some expectation must have been built up about potential high benefits to search, or else search costs must be truly trivial, in order for the potential incumbent to stand a chance of usurping the established firm.

This discussion has led us into the third and perhaps most important question: since the assumptions will generally be untrue, how robust are the results to minor modifications of the assumptions of the model? To put it another way, does 'almost perfectly contestable' mean anything? This is partly a technical and partly a practical question, and on the practical side it is rather too soon to give any judgement. On the technical side, the outcome may well be some way from what would be expected of perfect contestability, even if the assumptions approximate to the conditions I have outlined. The example used above draws upon models of the Diamond (1971)–Stiglitz (1979) type in which arbitrarily small search costs change outcomes substantially from those that would prevail with zero search costs. Other examples are provided by Schwartz and Reynolds (1983). Yet in their reply, Baumol et al. (1983) discuss equally plausible models in which the outcome does not suddenly differ from that obtaining when their conditions hold, as those conditions are relaxed.

All this is not to deny that perfect contestability provides a benchmark, moreover an extremely important one as we shall see shortly. But it does point out that 'almost perfectly contestable' may not have the same status as 'almost perfectly competitive'. This subject is raised again and treated at some length in a more empirical context in chapter 7.

Sustainability and entry barriers

A natural monopoly is sustainable if there is no vector of prices and associated vector of outputs which allow an incumbent's total costs to be at least covered by revenues but which make entry unattractive. Therefore the possibility of there being a natural monopoly is intimately related to the assumptions regarding potential entrant behaviour. Yet here, as Shepherd (1984) notes, there is a large divergence between the literature on barriers to entry, often assuming the Sylos postulate, and most of the literature on sustainability, which implicitly assumes perfect contestability.

If we suppose the industry is perfectly contestable, then exit is costless and entry is free, so a potential entrant faces only a negligible loss if things go wrong. Hence established-firm prices for the vector of products supplied may be expected to fall to average costs on average across the range, if the established firm is to remain in control. Thus, for example, a single-product natural monopoly operating at output levels on the falling portion of the average cost curve is only (price) sustainable at price equal to average cost.

The early literature on barriers to entry (e.g. Bain, 1956) emphasized structural features within the context of a specific behavioural assumption, the Sylos postulate. This puts the established firm in a more powerful position than the potential entrant, since the entrant believes the established firm's output is fixed. One consequence is that even scale economies arising through fixed costs create a substantial barrier to entry. In fact, in some cases fixed costs can enable the established firm to price as high as the monopoly level yet induce no entry — what Bain called 'blockaded entry' (see Dixit, 1979). Therefore, in such situations natural monopolies will be sustainable for many different prices. Positions like that associated with demand curve D_2 in figure 2.2 will be sustainable since the established firm is assumed by the potential entrant to continue supplying its existing amount to the market.[3]

The point may be made more general. There will be a set of natural monopoly markets sustainable as natural monopolies given specific pricing policies under the assumption of perfect contestability. There is a wider set of natural monopolies sustainable as natural monopolies either with specific pricing policies or in some cases under a wide range of pricing policies, given alternative assumptions regarding entry. The former group is a subset of the latter since if outputs and prices are sustainable to 'ultra-free' entry they will definitely be sustainable to less than free entry.

Without wanting to make things complicated for the sake of it, it is also worth pointing out that a natural monopoly market may be sustainable as, say, a duopoly, in conditions of less than free entry. An easy way to see this is to assume each firm faces a cost structure involving a constant marginal cost plus a fixed cost. This fixed cost makes the industry a natural monopoly − the more firms, the more fixed cost chunks are paid, and there are no offsetting advantages. Assume both firms are just breaking even at prevailing prices so neither wishes to leave. Given a Sylos assumption by a potential entrant, entry will seem nonsensical since price is bound to fall as the entrant's output will add to industry output, and the potential entrant (with the same technology as the established firm) will therefore make losses. Hence the presence of entry barriers may not mean there are too few firms in the industry, there may actually be too many (von Weizsäcker, 1980).

The point of this discussion is to bring out the important link between contestability and sustainability, a topic to which we shall return. Making a market more contestable can have various effects on sustainability, as has been illustrated above.

2.4 Invisible or visible hands?

So far in this chapter I have been gathering together pieces of analysis. Now is the time to begin fitting them together into the jigsaw, to demonstrate a powerful result extending the invisible hand beyond perfect competition to circumstances under which a natural monopoly has an efficient output

---

[3]The implications of this point for actual entry are discussed in chapter 7.

and pricing structure. In order that we can appreciate the result (and, ultimately, its limitations), let us first summarize the relationship between the pieces.

The first point to note is that, unlike sustainability and contestability, subadditivity and contestability are not necessarily linked. A perfectly competitive market is also perfectly contestable, but a natural monopoly may or may not be contestable (a question we shall look at shortly). Therefore, there is a set of natural monopoly industries and a set of perfectly contestable industries, and these sets, presumably, intersect (see figure 2.6).

Let us now introduce sustainability. Of the natural monopolies that are perfectly contestable, some will not be sustainable and some will be sustainable at specific prices, as we have seen. Of those that are not perfectly contestable, most will be sustainable as monopolies at *some* set of prices, though some may also be sustainable as duopolies, or whatever.[4] Increasing contestability is likely to make some natural monopolies not sustainable (e.g. the single-product rising cost cases), but in other cases the effect will be to discipline pricing behaviour more severely.

When considering the question of natural monopoly, we found some sufficient conditions for subadditivity, one of which was decreasing ray average cost plus transray convexity. Therefore it is likely that some, though not all, of the industries in the set of perfectly contestable natural monopolies will display decreasing ray average cost plus transray convexity.

Which industries out of this set will be sustainable? The Weak Invisible Hand Theorem states that 'Under a set of assumptions — includ[ing] a cost function exhibiting both economies of scale and transray convexity, Ramsey-optional price-output vectors are sufficient to guarantee sustainability' (Baumol et al., 1982, p. 209).[5] By implication at least some perfectly contestable natural monopolies are sustainable with Ramsey prices though others, admittedly, are not. (Note that the former set need not actually display Ramsey pricing, though Baumol et al. argue that this will in fact be the most straightforward thing for them to do.)

That set of industries which are natural monopolies, are perfectly contestable and are sustained using Ramsey prices, give rise to a socially very desirable result. All the advantages of natural monopoly are achieved and none of the disadvantages, because their pricing structure is optimal given the breakeven constraint. This provides a benchmark for evaluating natural monopoly industries, in the same way that perfect competition provides

---

[4]In addition, there will be a group of industries where entry is difficult which are sustainable as monopolies, though they are not natural monopolies.
[5]They extend the theorem beyond perfectly contestable markets.

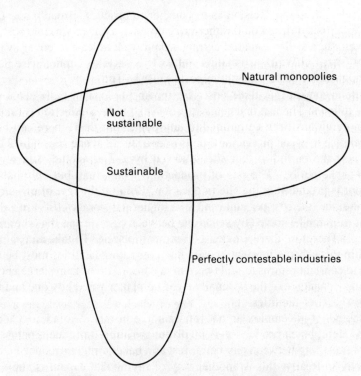

Natural monopolies

Not
sustainable

Sustainable

Perfectly contestable industries

Figure 2.6   Sustainability and contestability

a benchmark — something that it would be desirable to work towards as a policy goal.

This has a rather surprising implication. In principle, in some natural monopoly industries outside controls are superfluous. No controls on pricing are required as long as entry is completely free, so that any action on behalf of policy-makers should have the aim of making entry as free as possible. Because this does not fit with preconceived notions of, say, electricity distribution or the postal service, we will have to qualify the result in various ways, in order to realize the extent of its truth.

The most fundamental question is, do the two sets, namely natural monopolies and perfectly contestable industries, in fact intersect? Weitzman (1983) claims they do not. Perfect contestability, remember, assumes that any scale economies arise through fixed rather than sunk costs. The reason for this is straightforward, since if the established firm is in the position of already having sunk its fixed costs then it is naturally in a better position than the potential entrant, because the cost of the equipment is irrelevant to the decision as to whether to produce. Broadly speaking, the established firm would rather price down to average variable cost than leave, whereas the potential entrant would want at least to cover average total cost. But Weitzman claims that scale economies cannot arise purely through fixed costs; that these costs must be sunk.

The argument that fixed costs are incompatible with scale economies is as follows. The fact that costs are not sunk means production is timeless — nothing has been committed at any point. But then, there can be no difference between producing x units over a period at one site and $x/2$ units for half the period at that site followed by $x/2$ at another site for the rest of the period. The rate of production is the same, but only half the output is produced at the site in question. Because the rate of production is the same, the cost per unit cannot be higher. (If storage costs are a problem, they can be solved by switching between one site and the other more often.) Therefore there are constant returns to scale. To take an example, within this scheme it might be said that computing facilities must be subject to constant returns to scale because a consortium of firms large enough to take advantage of the optimally sized computer could buy one and then time-share its facilities.

Baumol et al. employ an aircraft example in their rejoinder to Weitzman. Here, batch production is involved: the aircraft produces batches of seats travelling between city pairs, just as a bakery might produce batches of loaves. Really, this is another way of saying that capital is sunk, but for a short period of time, because whilst the plane is in use it is not available for alternative flights. Deciding to enter the airline market between two points means at minimum hiring a plane for, say, one month, and within that period costs will be sunk. The point Baumol et al. are really making is that this period may seem trivially small compared, say, to the sinkage of capital involved in the decision to build and operate a power station.

Returning to the main theme, we have discovered that natural monopolies can coexist with *almost* perfectly contestable industries. To move on, within this set some industries will be sustainable, some will not be. We have already seen an example of a non-sustainable single-product case, involving rising average costs. As another (commonly quoted) example, we may take the Faulhaber (1975) case involving economies of scope.

Faulhaber's example has the following structure:

The cost of supplying any one of three communities with water, C(1), is   £300

The cost of supplying any two of the three communities, C(2), is   £400

The cost of supplying all three, C(3), is   £650

Notice that the cost structure is subadditive, i.e.

$$C(2) < 2C(1)$$
$$C(3) < C(2) + C(1) < 3C(1)$$

How will revenues be collected in order to support the natural monopoly in the supply of water? No one of the three communities A, B and C would be willing to pay more than £300 to join in a group scheme, since they could go it alone for £300. Similarly, no two communities would be willing to pay more than £400, since they could obtain a scheme for themselves for that amount. Hence representing revenues from community X by R(X) we can say:

$$R(A) + R(B) \leq 400$$
$$R(A) + R(C) \leq 400$$
$$R(B) + R(C) \leq 400$$

Summing and dividing by two:

$$R(A) + R(B) + R(C) \leq 600.$$

The consequence is that the group of three communities would not be willing to go for the scheme involving supply to all three, since they would not be able to come up with an agreed method of sharing the £650.

Faulhaber makes the point quite general. What we have been trying to do is to find 'subsidy-free' prices which will cover the costs of the enterprise. Such costs are less than go-it-alone costs, but are at least sufficient to cover the added costs of supplying the additional group or units of demand. Prices satisfying these costs are Pareto-superior to go-it-alone prices or prices for subgroups, so that it would seem people would be willing to pay them, yet in our example it turned out that they are not.

It is further easy to see that there is no necessary connection between subsidy-free prices and Ramsey-optional prices. The former depend for their structure upon the costs of alternative means of supply, whereas the latter, as we have seen, depend upon marginal costs and upon demand elasticities. Ramsey-optimal prices are not concerned with alternative means of supply: hence they are in principle susceptible to competitive entry.

A simple example (drawing on Mirman, Tauman and Zang, 1986) will make the point. Assume that the cost function of a multiproduct firm is completely separable (no economies/diseconomies of scope etc.). Then the only possible sustainable prices are average cost (not Ramsey) prices, since they are equivalent to go-it-alone prices from efficient new entrants. (But, as we saw in the Faulhaber example, not all average cost prices are sustainable in general.) Of course the Mirman et al. example does not involve a natural monopoly, yet those authors are able to generalize it to show that certain *average* cost price vectors are sustainable.

Looking at things from this viewpoint, it is perhaps surprising that the 'invisible hand' theorem works at all. But we also gain insight into when it will work, namely in cases (unlike Faulhaber's and Mirman et al.'s) where cost conditions sufficient to prevent the possibility of competitive entry are imposed. Hence the theorem can only be valid under rather specific assumptions on industry cost structure.

2.5 Concluding remarks

The efforts of Baumol et al. have resulted in substantial clarification of the theory of natural monopoly. Moreover, their viewpoint has had a considerable impact upon practical regulatory policy. Their insight that the reduction of entry barriers will, in some cases, suffice to force a natural monopoly into quasi-competitive behaviour was one element underlying the continuing experiment in airline deregulation in the United States (charted in chapter 7).

Nevertheless, this same body of theory has also shown that it is quite possible in some cases for entry to destroy natural monopoly properties, as in the Faulhaber example above. Here then, there is a perfectly legitimate case for restriction of entry, in order to impose the one-supplier situation which is welfare-preferred yet is not forthcoming through the workings of the invisible hand.

We can go further. Supply of a set of goods within a natural monopoly framework may under some circumstances require suppression of entry into closely related areas in order to prevent competitive entry undermining the natural monopoly properties. Von Weizsäcker (1984) gives the example of a natural monopoly transport sector with public provision being undermined by competitive entry in the area of private cars. Cost-based prices would prevent such entry, but would probably require a subsidy. The point is that the set of products which are socially relevant to the group-optimality calculation may not coincide with the set which are actually controlled by the firm in question. Despite recent insights then, a respectable case can be made out for some form of intervention in some natural monopoly cases.

Apart from cases such as those we have been discussing, where the industries are nearly perfectly contestable, there are other, more traditional cases where the industry is a natural monopoly but a long way from being naturally contestable. Here Ramsey-optimal prices might be charged by the incumbent, but there is no particularly compelling reason to suggest that they will be, in the absence of intervention. Hence there is a case for intervention in terms of regulating prices and conditions of supply.

It should be said at this stage that the case for regulation in any situation is weakened to the extent that the institutions which will themselves be involved are imperfect. Thus in chapters 4 to 6 we discuss alternative institutional structures.

Finally, and more generally, it may perhaps be worthwhile to spell out the ways in which production may not match up to ideals under either regulation or unfettered market operation. Prices not in line with Ramsey-optimal ones or not in line with costs are not necessarily the most important problem. Equally important in achieving desirable results may be attaining the correct number of products from the point of view of variety, the correct extent of vertical and horizontal product differentiation between the variants, etc. These matters have, unfortunately, been only little explored[6] and prescriptions are less easy to write.

Notes on the literature

The key source for much of the material of this chapter, particularly the cost concepts, is Baumol, Panzar and Willig (1982). A somewhat easier guide to parts of it is Sharkey (1982). Shepherd (1984) provides a rather unfocused critique of much of this work, whilst a useful review is Brock (1984). Von Weizsäcker's (1984) thoughtful paper clarifies some of the pricing issues. On Ramsey pricing itself, the classic reference is Baumol and Bradford (1970). A review of the cost concepts is provided by Bailey and Friedlaender (1982) and for the reader interested in the practical use of these concepts, Friedlaender et al. (1983) provides an extensive illustration for the US motor industry. The paper by Stiglitz (1979) provides an overview of equilibria when there is imperfect information. Finally, for more recent overviews of contestability theory, see Baumol and Willig (1986) and Schwartz (1986).

---

[6]For a model along these lines, see, for example, Telser (1969).

3

Regulation and the Theory of the Firm

Are regulated and unregulated firms likely to be equally efficient? Arguably not. In many ways, a regulated firm is just like any other. In any large firm the managers have considerable scope for indulging in actions which may not be in the best interests of the owners, or for allowing their subordinates a freer rein than might be in the owners' interests. Yet at the same time, managers face constraints on their actions. It seems natural to assert that the extent to which managers deviate from owners' interests will depend upon the degree of scope available to them and the degree to which they are constrained. Thus the firm's constraint structure can affect its behaviour on pricing and its costs.

From this viewpoint, we have to modify our analysis of the regulatory system in certain ways. In chapter 2, we thought of the firm's costs as parametrically determined (and hence we focused on prices), but they are not. Costs are endogenously determined along with many other things within the firm. Hence even a specific target, say 'price to cover average costs', can be met in many ways, because average costs may be high because the firm is relatively inefficient, or low because it is relatively efficient. Cost efficiency is a key factor.

The message for this chapter is that the questions we are asking about firm structures have to be comparative institutional ones. As Spence (1975) says, 'the firm, in large part, consists of nonmarket institutions whose function is to deal with resource allocation in the presence of informational constraints that markets handle poorly or do not handle at all' (p. 164). Different institutions may well have different costs and different maximands due to differing efficiencies or other strengths, but there is no absolute standard of efficiency, because of the informational constraints.

The purpose of this chapter is to examine the comparative institutional questions concerning which types of firm structure may be relatively efficient, and which relatively inefficient. I shall do this by considering what mechanisms may be involved in forming the constraint structure on the firm, prior to any regulatory constraints being imposed. Thus although it is recognized that regulatory agencies can influence behaviour, it is also true that the framework on to which they impose constraints is not the same regardless of the underlying institutional structure.

It will be revealed that there is the potential for both publicly owned and publicly regulated concerns to perform less efficiently than public liability companies in the absence of external constraints. Essentially, there are three key features which may differ as between an open or public liability corporation (plc), a publicly regulated corporation and a publicly owned corporation. First, there is the external constraint structure. Secondly there is the mechanism which determines top management emoluments, implicit in which is their incentive structure. Thirdly, there is the internal relationship between management and employees. In each of these cases my method will be to discuss the effects the phenomenon has upon public liability companies, then to make comparison with the other forms in which we are interested. Thus the specific control structures to be discussed in chapters 4 to 6 can be put into context.

The comparative institutional analysis outlined above proceeds as follows. In order to keep things manageable, section 3.1 is devoted entirely to explaining the external constraint structure bearing on a plc, while section 3.2 provides the comparisons between plc's and alternative institutions. The managerial emolument and incentives discussion in section 3.3 starts in general terms and then moves to questions of alternative institutional structures. Section 3.4 provides a rather briefer coverage of internal relationships, whilst section 3.5 contains some concluding remarks. An appendix demonstrates the importance of striving to keep costs to efficient levels, a topic relevant to this and to several subsequent chapters.

3.1 Potential external constraints on a plc's managers

One school of thought has it that managers of large private corporations are more or less their own masters (Berle and Means, 1932). The theoretical owners of the firm, namely the shareholders, are by and large passive and essentially dependent upon management, who know more about the firm than anyone else. Hence the chief executive is able to maximize his/her own utility (Williamson, 1963) as long as the shareholders get some basic, probably low, return.

There is little doubt that there is some truth in this story, but more recently it has been recognized (see for example, Jensen and Meckling, 1976) that modelling the behaviour of the chief executive without thought as to the behaviour of other actors in the firm is naive. These others include the shareholders and outside interests such as banks etc., but also inside interests, junior managers and operatives, for example. In order properly to analyse the performance of the firm, we must also take account of these considerations. Having examined the position in general terms, the insights will be used in the next section to gain a perspective on the situation in regulated and public concerns.

To take an example, the observation that shareholders are on the whole behaving passively is consistent with the view that they know little about the firm and consequently leave everything to the manager. But then, we might ask, whey entrust money to the manager? The shareholders could also be passive because the manager is doing precisely what they require for high returns on that money. More sensibly, it is quite possible that the manager is not earning returns as high as shareholders would like, yet that because it is costly for shareholders to gain enough additional information to improve the situation sufficiently to make it worthwhile whilst acting rationally, they appear passive.

This example illustrates the essential idea of modelling the behaviour of other actors associated with the firm, as well as that of the managers. The general framework adopted is a 'principal–agent' one, the manager being the agent of principals such as the shareholders. There seems no particular reason to ascribe economic rationality to one group and not the other. But then we have to consider how each of these other groups or forces impact upon the firm.

To return to the shareholder example, having raised the point that it is in shareholders' interests to ensure their returns are reasonable, it logically follows that there will be an incentive for them to spend a certain amount of time and money finding out about the firm's activities and performance. Presumably, the rational shareholder would do this up to the point at which marginal benefit was equated with marginal cost. However, we then have to acknowledge that the marginal benefit to any individual shareholder without a controlling interest is likely to be very small.

The only real way that a shareholder can exercise an interest is by threatening to depose incumbent management if performance does not improve. But in order to do this, it is necessary to have the backing of a majority of the shareholders who would vote on the issue (not necessarily a majority of the shareholders). Either other people must simultaneously be gathering information, or the shareholder will have to collect enough information to convince others. However there is a free rider problem. Because all shareholders will benefit if performance improves (either through usurping present management or by frightening them into improved performance), why should any rational individual be the one to incur the costs; why not leave it to someone else? The presence of this free rider problem does not mean that no resources will be devoted to shareholder monitoring behaviour, but it does mean that the resources devoted will be sub-optimal from the viewpoint of shareholders as a group.

So, shareholders cannot be relied upon necessarily to provide much of a constraint on managers. Can the firm's bankers? Any loan from the bank involves a risk of default, and the bank will be concerned about this even though it has sought security from the firm. Even if the security is ample, the bank will not want the time, trouble and loss of goodwill involved in attempting to repossess its loan. Hence the bank will want to keep the risk of default low. The bank is unconcerned, however, about how good performance *could be*: all it is interested in is performance being good *enough* to make the loan fairly secure. Hence, although banks provide a constraint, they do not ensure efficiency. In fact, if anything, the bank's constraint on managers seems the most like that modelled in Baumol (1959), Williamson (1963) etc. − that is, a minimum profit constraint. But this is known to lead to results that differ from profit maximization in general.

There are other constraints on the firm's capital, however, most importantly perhaps, the takeover constraint. The basic idea is fairly simple; that individual shareholders, disappointed with the firm's performance, gradually decide to sell their shares rather than attempt to surmount the free rider problem discussed earlier. With this, the market price falls to well below potential value. The way is then clear for an astute outside agent to purchase shares, realizing their potential and current values are far apart, and subsequently to make a bid for the remainder, with the eventual aim either of realizing the company's assets, or putting in new management, and hence getting a return on the investment. If this constraint is important in reality, that is if sufficient outside individuals or firms are actively considering opportunities, then it would seem the only way to avoid takeover is to employ the company's assets efficiently.

Yet again, things are not this straightforward. The mere signal of takeover intentions normally engenders a rise in the share price, hence a lessening in the advantages of selling out to another party. Share values are assumed to reflect the stream of future earnings obtainable from them, but the future is unknown (though shareholders naturally have expectations). Hence current management has an incentive to suggest that information they have (presumably private to them or not previously sufficiently appreciated) suggests a rosy future under the present regime. The takeover raider suggests the opposite. But such activities − advertising and the like − are costly, and the raider may have to improve the offer in order to get sufficient shareholders to agree, which lessens the raider's own return. In addition, institutional factors have an impact. Obviously if the potential raider can price discriminate, that is catch some shareholders unaware, at a low price, and gradually buy from others at gradually increasing prices, this will be advantageous to the raider. However, the Takeover Code in the UK, for example, acts to enforce equal treatment of the shareholdings to be acquired once a critical small percentage of shares has been obtained. The final ruling price is paid to all. This reduces the advantage to the raider, and so too the likelihood of a takeover.

Therefore the view that none of the capital market constraints by itself will ensure efficiency is clearly defensible. What, then, about the product market? Specifically, it seems plausible that if there is extensive competition in the market, relatively inefficient firms will be forced out. In monopoly situations, where there is no competition, what has been called 'X-inefficiency' (Leibenstein, 1966; Crew, Jones-Lee and Rowley, 1971) can be claimed to arise without necessitating exit.

Of course, we must recall that the textbook model of perfect competition abstracts from important aspects of reality such as imperfect information and costly monitoring by shareholders and others. Hence with our present framework perfect competition does not necessarily imply an efficient set of firms. Nevertheless, it would seem sensible to say that, given a set of firms in a perfectly competitive market, some of which (perhaps because of a more concentrated distribution of shares) face quite tight constraints on their efficiency, these relatively efficient firms are likely to provide some form of policing function over the others. For example, they may force the potentially inefficient firms either to join them in adopting cost-saving innovations which involve some disruption of current working practices, or to go to the wall. This policing function is less likely to be present in the case of a monopolist, which does not face direct product market pressure. Therefore there may well be something in the view that the product market imposes a constraint, though not in the extreme version that perfect competition is synonymous with efficiency.

The last major constraint, and the one we will examine in most detail, is peer group pressure on the managers themselves, or the operation of the managerial labour market. Managers invest a large amount of human capital in the firms that employ them. Hence, arguably, they wish to see a return on that investment. This can come from current emoluments or some other source. In fact, managers could take it in non-pecuniary terms – in the (1963) Williamsonian manner. However, Fama (1980) would argue that this is shortsighted. The firm can adjust subsequent managerial salaries to reflect overconsumption of non-salary perquisites, or at least can attempt to do so based on the information available. Thus in principle there exist mechanisms for *ex post* settling up.

I introduced above the idea of a managerial labour market in the context of the salary package setting procedure. Presumably when the (outside?) directors of the company meet they will discuss the earnings of the top managerial staff, and attempt to keep them in line with the manager's worth (marginal product) to the company. However, the concept can be extended to cover the external as well as the internal managerial labour market, and for present purposes this is the more important aspect.

The alternative for a manager if he does not like what is on offer in his present job is to move to a different one. It is here that another strand of Fama's argument comes in. How is the new firm to assess the manager's likely worth to them? There are bound to be factors other than visible qualifications which influence this. One signal of worth is current pay, another is perceived performance in the current post. Assuming these signals convey useful information, it is not optimal for a manager to 'rip off' the current firm hoping to move on to another very shortly, because the second firm will pick up some hint of this behaviour, any subsequent firm a stronger hint, and so on.

Moreover, the immediate benefits that the manager gains in a firm by lowering his *ex post* marginal product below the *ex ante* one are likely to be outweighed by the losses to the firm as a result, if only because this manager is a member of a team whose marginal products are interdependent. Therefore, if there is full *ex post* settling up, the manager is likely to end up worse off than if he had not deviated from the accepted behaviour.

The managerial labour market thus has both an internal and an external dimension. Arguably it provides a very strong constraint on managers to act efficiently, if we may assume they are concerned about their future career path and if they believe that the firm does not systematically assess their performance wrongly.

Before concluding the development of this framework, we should investigate the relationship between the constraints. Specifically, is it necessary for all the constraints to operate effectively in order for the firm's manager(s) to run the firm efficiently? Smirlock and Marshall (1983) take the view that each set of constraints excepting the product market is in principle a sufficient condition for efficient performance: 'If any of these mechanisms [competition among managers, owners' design and monitoring of incentive schemes, capital markets] ... were to operate perfectly (and costlessly), then, regardless of the output market environment, profit maximisation would be coincident with utility maximisation by managers' (p. 168). Thus, an efficient managerial labour market would be enough.

A rather different view is given by Stiglitz (1985): 'There are systematic biases associated with each of the control mechanisms ...' (p. 146). Specifically, he notes that lenders like banks have an interest in the firm's

undertaking projects that carry little risk of default even if the expected
return is low, whilst if it is true that shareholders in general hold diversified portfolios, they would want the firm to go for high expected returns.
Therefore, banks and shareholders (or, at least the large institutional
shareholders plus unit trust holders etc.) do not have the same objectives.
They would want to constrain the manager in different ways.

In addition, as Stiglitz points out, the managerial labour market is not
necessarily the powerful constraining force many believe it to be; biases
exist there also. In particular, reward structures are unlikely to be correlated with long-term returns; in fact managerial compensation is likely
to be based on performance over a two- or three-year period. Yet of course
many projects do not come to fruition for very many years, and large
important projects lead to adverse short-term cash flows. Managers are
naturally biased towards projects showing a quick return, if they feel there
is unlikely to be *ex post* settling up over the longer term.

Thus Stiglitz sees the control problem as a multiple-principal–single-
agent problem with each principal having a somewhat different objective.
There is almost bound to be incentive incompatibility between principals
and agent as a consequence. No single control mechanism can ensure
efficiency.

3.2 Differing constraints in different institutional structures

I have dwelt on the potential capital market and other outside constraints
on the plc in order to provide a standpoint from which to view the constraints operating in those cases which are more our concern. Differing
constraint structures, we might expect, will make for different performance.

It is possible to devise a scheme representing (maybe, caricaturing) various
institutional structures; an example is given in table 3.1.[1] This deliberately covers a broad range of six types of structure, across five different
possible constraints, in summary form. A plus indicates an important constraint, a minus the constraint's absence. The basis is the plc taken as a
paradigm in the previous section. We have assumed that the product market
provides very little by way of constraint in this case in order to bring out
the important point that comparisons should be like-with-like. To pursue
the point, although it is normal for regulated companies and publicly owned
companies to face little competition, if they were replaced by some other

[1]Similar types of tables are presented in Forsyth (1984) and Kay and Thompson (1986).
There will always be minor classification disagreements – see Prowse (1986).

Table 3.1 Controls on managers in different institutional structures

Constraint	Public liability company (plc)	Limited company	Partnership	Non-profit mutual institutions	Regulated company	Public authority owned company
Product market	− (?)	− (?)	− (?)	− (?)	− (?)	− (?)
Shareholders	+	+	+	− (?)	− (?)	−
Stock market (takeovers etc.)	+	−	−	−	− (?)	−
Bankruptcy	+	+	+	− (?)	− (?)	−
External managerial labour market	+	+	+	+	+	+

structure it is not clear that competition would develop. Because of the industries they tend to occupy, partnerships and 'non-profits' (e.g. solicitors and building societies, respectively), also often face only limited competition.

Moving to the capital market constraints, the takeover constraint is more or less unique to public liability companies though even then it cannot impact strongly on the very largest companies. Closed shareholding companies (e.g. family owned ones) are obviously not subject to (involuntary) takeovers, neither are most mutuals and non-profits. Nor, for practical purposes, are they a constraint for *most* regulated public companies given their size and their controlled returns. Shareholders (assuming we take the partners in a partnership to be shareholders) potentially provide a constraint in some cases; in fact this constraint may be stronger in partnerships and limited companies than in public liability companies. The shareholders in non-profit institutions and publicly owned companies in both cases are more or less synonymous with the customers of the firm; they provide no additional constraint apart from this, though in publicly owned companies the relevant government department will impose its own constraints (see chapter 4). Indeed, if the state can be thought of as acting as a single shareholder then it will be in a more powerful position *vis-à-vis* management than are shareholders of most private companies. In the case of bankruptcy, partnerships clearly feel more constrained, since their unlimited liability means the owner/managers have more to lose than in any other case; they will tend to be risk-averse. Bankruptcy is assumed here to be a most unlikely event in non-profits, regulated companies and publicly owned companies, though this may be influenced by the action of the regulatory agency.[2]

Finally, we come to the managerial labour market constraint. Here, assuming managers move or can move between company types, this constraint potentially bears on all cases. Certainly, *some* movement (in the UK) takes place between publicly owned and public liability companies, and one imagines there is some movement between, say, mutual (i.e. non-profit) insurance companies and public liability insurance companies. Similarly, accountants, say, move between chartered accountancy partnerships and industry. Thus in no case can a potential manager's career path be said to lie necessarily within one column of the table. Therefore, in performing within an institution in one category the manager may bear in mind his/her marketability in another area.

It will not have escaped notice that minuses predominate towards the

---

[2]For example, Bailey et al. (1985) suggest that the actions of the US Civil Aeronautics Board greatly reduced the probability of bankruptcy amongst those they regulated.

right hand side of the table. Does this imply that inferior performance can be expected in these structures? This at least partly depends on the relationship between the constraints. If one were to take Smirlock and Marshall's view (1983) that any one constraint is sufficient for efficient company performance, and if managers do perceive that career paths can involve movement between various company types, then an efficient managerial labour market constraint would suffice to promote efficiency in *any* structural type. From a policy point of view, if in any specific area regulated company and public authority company managers were not commonly recruited from outside, this line of argument would suggest that outside applications should be encouraged.

On the other hand, if one were to take the Stiglitz line (1985), things would not be as clear-cut. A plus in the managerial labour market row in table 3.1 is no longer sufficient, but nor is it necessarily true that the more pluses the better; each constraint pushes the manager in a particular way. Because of this, it is useful to obtain a different perspective.

We now come to the reason for including partnerships and non-profits in the table, even though these structures are not really our concern. The point is that they provide an institutional contrast to public liability companies which, unlike regulated and publicly owned companies, occur naturally (without governmental interference) in advanced capitalist societies. Therefore they shed light on the comparative institutional questions with which we are concerned. Specifically, one strong hypothesis is that of Fama and Jensen: 'Organisations compete for survival, and the form of organisation that survives in an activity is the one that delivers the product demanded by the customers at the lowest price while covering costs' (1983a, p. 345) — a Darwinian view.[3]

Fama and Jensen's view (1983a, b) is that partnerships, even large partnerships, and various forms of non-profit organizations like mutual financial companies, survive as organizational forms because they have particular strengths. In general terms, within the particular situations, those structures provide economical ways of performing decision management (initiating decisions and implementing them) and decision control (ratifying decisions and monitoring them).

In the case of the large professional partnership, Fama and Jensen argue that the shareholders in such a firm have enough knowledge about its activities to be able to protect their interests, without either the need to all be on the board, or to have recourse to external representatives. The board

---

[3]Though this is in one sense a strong hypothesis, that the strongest survive and the weakest go to the wall, it is in another sense a weak one, because it is not clear how it could be refuted.

(the managing partners) makes the decisions about who should be admitted to the partnership, who removed, what their share should be and so on, but there is complex mutual control over this group. Therefore the strength of the partnership as a form presumably lies in the large amount of shared knowledge about the business arising from the nature of the people employed in it, that is, in the special nature of its shareholders. Individual agents may be willing to submit to mutual monitoring because it is likely to reduce fluctuations in the value of their human capital.

Turning now to financial mutuals, the key feature Fama and Jensen see here is that residual claims are redeemable on demand. Therefore, if people do not like the decisions management is taking, they will withdraw their funds, something which is easier in a financial firm than in most others. This, arguably, provides a diffuse but important form of decision control over the managers. The threat of liquidation by 'shareholders' is far more potent than in other forms, and it brings with it the threat that management will have no assets to manage.

In fact, this specific case is particularly relevant since in insurance two forms of companies coexist (in the UK), mutuals and public liability companies. Moreover, the former often outperform the latter; consumer magazines commonly suggest specific mutual companies as providing the best deal and there is some evidence that they are superior in performance more generally (see, for example, Finsinger, 1983). Perhaps the combination of shareholder and customer roles in one body is a source of particular strength. In summary, whether or not Fama and Jensen's reasoning is right, it cannot be said that more minuses in table 3.1 mean worse performance.

Returning from our detour, what, if anything, can be said about regulated and publicly owned companies compared with public liability companies? First that, in the absence of special strengths, and on the basis of external restraints, we might expect such companies to perform worse than a plc. Secondly, if the managerial labour constraint is powerful, performance may not be very much worse. Thirdly, since there are additional elements of control which are germane, the question of relative performance cannot be decided on a priori grounds. It may, for example, vary from country to country (see Perotin and Estrin, 1986).

One possible special factor is that in small local communities, monitoring of performance by consumers/voters may take on an important role. It need not take much effort to write to the local paper, or phone a councillor, with a complaint, and the effects will impact upon management. The direction in which management will be pushed need not be a more efficient one (for example, more money might be allocated to controlling conspicuous waste than is justified economically), but the potency of the control is fairly obvious.

In addition to the external controls, factors internal to the firm also matter, both to the firm's overall efficiency and, therefore, also to its ability to survive. External bodies may be able to keep management from moving in undesirable directions, but can they also ensure that detailed internal decisions and management procedures run smoothly? Again, there are general comparative institutional differences which can be identified. Let us turn to this question.

3.3 The firm's internal relationships: managerial emoluments

Shareholders, banks and so on do not necessarily tightly constrain managers essentially because they lack enough information to do so, and this is either a result of some problem in the market for information (e.g. the public good problem amongst shareholders) or because the information is inherently difficult to obtain. Similar problems arise in decisions about how and what to pay managers, and how and what to pay employees. One of the major factors creating difficulties in obtaining information is randomness in the external environment facing the firm. Such uncertainty also means that risk characteristics of the actors under consideration become important. We now turn to examining the interlinkages between uncertainty, information and effort.

People are normally considered to be risk-averse over amounts of the order of magnitude of their incomes. For example, virtually all university lecturers, if asked to choose concerning next year's pay between two deals, the first being this year's pay (adjusted for inflation) and the second a 50 per cent random chance of nothing and 50 per cent chance of double this year's (inflation-adjusted) pay, would opt for the former. Such people have a concave utility of income function, i.e.

$$U = U(I) \qquad U' > 0 \qquad U'' < 0 \tag{3.1}$$

Amongst them there will be people who are more or less risk-averse at any given income. One convenient way to represent this is by using the Pratt–Arrow concept of absolute risk aversion, $RA = -U''/U'$. The larger this magnitude, the more risk-averse the person. Thus in figure 3.1 two individuals, A and B, are represented by utility of income functions between £0 and £1000. At the £500 certain income level, they are constructed to have the same slope (and the same slope as has the curve labelled C, which would be appropriate for a risk-neutral person). However, A displays more curvature than B at that point, and hence more risk aversion.

We may also consider the value to A and to B of a bet, say for a simple example a 50 per cent chance of £0 and a 50 per cent chance of £1000. The expected value of any bet such as this is given by the appropriate point on line C, and reading across from point X to curve A reveals that this gamble is only worth £210 with certainty to A, and £400 likewise to B. Thus suppose A were to win a lottery ticket carrying a 50 per cent chance of £1000, it could be sold to B for, say, £300 and both would feel better off (before the final outcome had been revealed).

This brings us to the concept of risk-sharing. It seems clear that, because they probably do not have as much of their total assets dependent upon the fortunes of a specific firm, the firm's shareholders are less risk-averse than the manager. In particular, the manager has a large amount of human capital invested in the firm which is difficult to hedge against so that he will be concerned about the possibility of very low earnings. Suppose the firm's income consists of a 50 per cent chance of £2000 and a 50 per cent chance of nothing. The owners consider offering the manager (suppose like A in figure 3.1), an income of £0 if the firm does badly, £1000 if it does well, 'contract 1', pocketing the rest themselves. The actual business of managing involves no loss of utility (we assume for simplicity), though the owner cannot do it. But the manager would rather be offered £211 every year, 'contract 2', whatever the outcome rather than contract 1. This

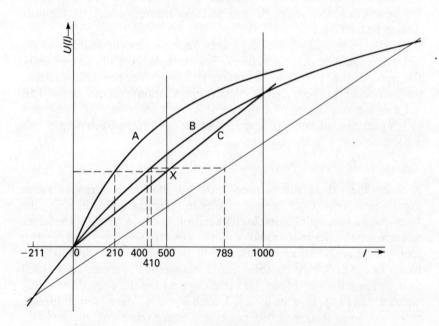

Figure 3.1   Risk aversion and the value of gambles

would mean the owner getting either $-£211$ or $£1789$, depending on the state of the world, a mean expectation of £789. Assume the owner is of type B. We have extended B's utility function and drawn in the line joining $-£211$ and $£1789$ to get the expected income. Reading across from £789, we find B would value this at about the equivalent of £410, whilst the alternative certainty equivalent under contract 1 is £400, as we saw previously (because the owner gets £0 or £1000 under contract 1). Hence the owner also would find it worthwhile acceding to contract 2 rather than contract 1.

Now it will not always be the case that it is optimal for the less risk-averse party to take on all the risk. Different curvatures would give different results in the sense that it would often be optimal for the more risk-averse to have some small part of the risk. In fact, in the case drawn, there are contracts involving some sharing which are superior. For example, both would appear to be better served by a contract which gave A £100 or £500, hence B $-£100$ or £1500 (this has not been drawn in, to avoid obscuring the main points of the figure). However, it will certainly be true that it is optimal for a risk-neutral party to take all risk from a risk-averse party (try A or B bargaining with C) and it would seem sensible that a more risk-averse party should optimally take on less of the risk than a less risk-averse one. Therefore, it seems shareholders should absorb the risks of an enterprise in preference to management doing so.

At this stage we must introduce another complication. The model we used above was very simple in that the manager, in effect, had only to toss the coin to determine the outcome. But of course managers manage; they take decisions and control factors of production. Moreover, it is difficult for anyone but the manager to have available all the information he or she has taken into account at the point of decision, and hence it is difficult to monitor the manager. The randomness of the environment has an important influence.

To see the impact of this, let us consider two examples. In the first, suppose the firm is undertaking a particular project. There is a 0.5 probability of success for the project available naturally. However, by making further efforts to improve certain facets of the project, the manager could increase this probability to 0.7. Unfortunately for the shareholders, the manager's effort is unobservable; all they see is whether the project succeeds or fails. Therefore, assuming the manager gets paid the same whether the project is a success of not, that manager has an incentive not to try very hard. This problem is sometimes called *moral hazard*, by analogy with insurance where the phenomenon is well known. If you insure all the property in your flat against theft, fire etc. you have less of an incentive to make the place thief-proof and to check over it carefully before going out or going to bed than if you were not insured. It can be very difficult for the insurance company, after the event, to ascertain what precautions were taken so that, in many cases, they will pay out however you behaved.[4] Arrow (1984) calls the general phenomenon *hidden action*, since what is not observed by the principal in general is the action of the agent, be it effort or whatever.

In the second example, suppose a specific project is under consideration and the manager, but no one else, knows there is a 0.7 probability it will yield a return of 20 per cent on the investment, with a 0.3 probability that it will yield nothing. If the firm's decision criterion is to go ahead if the expected return is 10 per cent, then it should go ahead. Another project, a pet project of the manager, has a 0.45 probability of yielding 20 per cent and a 0.55 chance of yielding nothing. The company should decide against this one. Clearly then, if the company is to choose one it should opt for the first. Suppose the manager instead goes ahead on the second. if it turns out well, the result is better for him than if the first option was followed. If it turns out badly, he might argue (contrary to the facts) that this was against the odds. The board of directors is unlikely to be in as good a position as the manager to judge on this. This phenomenon also arises in the field of insurance where it is known as *adverse selection*. On average, the people who are most likely to opt for health insurance are those who know themselves to be relatively unhealthy. More generally, Arrow (1984) calls it *hidden information* or *hidden knowledge* – the principal does not know all that the agent knows.

Faced with these potential problems, what can be done? The insurance company can check *ex post* in some cases (after a theft) or it can screen prior to accepting risk (health insurance). Both are costly. Alternatively, it can refuse to accept the whole risk – this is common in car insurance and it happens in practice after thefts in which a considerable mess is created.[5]

Shareholders can likewise impose some or all of these constraints on the manager. A manager's pay often is not a fixed salary but contains a bonus element dependent upon performance (profitability etc.). The 'package' may also involve stock options – rights to buy shares at a specific value exercisable at a future date, the idea being that if the firm does well the shares will be worth far more than the exercise price. In this case,

---

[4]Of course, the problem can get out of hand. Most bicycle insurers insist that bicycles are locked to something and may refuse to pay if it transpires they were not.

[5]If there are several contracts available, some involving the company in more risk than others, then customer self-selection is equivalent to *ex ante* screening.

the shareholders are passing off some risk on to the manager. Alternatively, or in addition, the manager's performance may be assessed against some criteria after a reasonable period has elapsed. It is one thing to say that individual projects failed 'against the odds'; it is more suspicious if they are always doing so. To put this another way, the larger the sample of observations, the smaller the variance and hence the more accurately inferences can be drawn.[6] And of course, firms indulge in screening prior to taking managers on, though relying upon references is probably rather a weak screen.

Returning to our earlier theme, we notice there is a tradeoff for shareholders' representatives in employing a manager. Managers are relatively risk-averse when compared with them, so on this count (intuitively), risk should lie mainly with shareholders. When it does, however, there are relatively poor incentives for managers to perform well. One straightforward way of providing incentives is to push some of the risk of poor performance on to managers.[7] Notice that what is being passed on *is* partly pure risk − the chance that, despite the manager's very best endeavours, things will go badly for the firm. The manager is master only of his actions, not the outcomes of those actions. Therefore there is a real tradeoff involved, between the need for any bonus to be relatively generous when compared with a flat salary, and the need for there to be some bonus element.

How should, and how do, managerial 'emoluments' differ between public liability companies, regulated companies and publicly owned companies? The scheme for managerial pay set out above essentially refers to the pay framework for a manager in a plc, but my aim is to provide a comparative analysis. In practice, managers of regulated companies, in the UK, have emoluments packages which appear similar to those enjoyed by purely private sector companies. Hence, I shall focus on pay in public concerns.

Managers in public industries are often paid quite differently from those in private industry. There is a far greater emphasis on basic salary than on bonus; indeed, in the UK until recently all managers of the major nationalized industries were paid the same (low, by private industry standards) salary − see also chapter 4. Perquisites are probably at a relatively low level, with the exception of the pension. Stock option schemes are not available either. Finally, the contract is often a fixed period one. On the other hand, we might somewhat irreverently say that *ex post* settling

---

[6]An instructive analogy is Stigler's (1964) 'Theory of oligopoly'.
[7]Demski (1976) demonstrates in general that when both parties are risk-averse, some risk-sharing is desirable.

up — in the form of a higher probability of honours (knighthoods etc.) than in private industry — provides some compensation.

Concerning the question of how emoluments *should* differ, the first point to make is that the reward structure in public industries should not ape that in the private sector. There are at least two reasons for this. First, the state arguably has the most widely diversified portfolio of any shareholder.[8] Hence the state, if anything can, should be classed as risk-neutral. Consequently (Demski, 1976 and other authors) it is inefficient for it to force on to the manager any general risk if this can be avoided, though the manager should still have some reward/penalty dependent upon his or her actions. If the actions cannot be independently observed at all though, this might force the optimal contract to contain some element based on general risk, in order to provide incentives to efficiency. It is often possible, however (as in the insurance company examples), to get some independent evidence of effort or actions. This might be direct (inquiries into 'what went wrong' which include examination of internal memoranda by the principal — it is easiest to think of the military example of courts martial) or indirect (examination of a run of decisions to assess their quality). This evidence can then be used to modify the contract or allow it to terminate and not to offer renewal. Here, the fixed period contract is very useful, if proper evaluation procedures are devised.

The second, perhaps more important, issue takes us back to points discussed in chapters 1 and 2, and it is relevant to the work reported in chapter 5. Monopoly power can often be exercised. Therefore, *financial* performance criteria are relatively easily met by raising prices sufficiently above costs, if allowed, or permitting service to deteriorate in order to make cost savings. These outcomes are most undesirable, just as they are in a purely private company. Indeed, imposing performance-based emoluments of this sort flies in the face of one major reason for regulation or public ownership in the first place.

This implies that bonuses or other discretionary awards should be based as far as possible on efficiency criteria — for example, the percentage by which constant service level costs have been reduced, and other productivity measures. Of course there are dangers here; we get into the problem that directives impose rigidity. If a manager is told to increase some measure of productivity, the manager will tend to distort things in just that direction. We all know the well-worn apocryphal stories of Soviet nail manufacturers told to maximize tons of nails produced per man and making them all large in order to do this most easily. Yet as we shall see in chapters

[8]The same could not be said however, for local authorities and enterprises under their control.

4 and 5, there has been considerable theoretical work (e.g. by Finsinger and Vogelsang, 1981) on socially efficient bonus structures, relating pay to social surplus created.

Where management rewards in publicly owned concerns are *institutionally* determined, we should expect such concerns to perform less well than privately owned firms in which salaries relate to performance. There is another point here. I argued earlier that the external managerial labour market is a potentially important constraint on managerial performance in the public (and regulated) sectors. It cannot be so if the managers are drawn from a different pool, which can happen if emoluments in the private sector drift too far away from those in the public sector. But a manager who meets targets, whether or not they are financial, is increasing his or her future prospects, so the constraints of the managerial labour market can be brought to bear.

3.4 Relationships between management and employees

The standard way to think of the manager–employee relationship is again as principal and agent respectively, though as we will see shortly, the relationship can be reversed. In these relationships, both parties are likely to be risk-averse, perhaps employees more so than the manager as they may have a greater proportion of human and other capital tied up in firm-specific assets.[9]

There are two facets to the manager/principal–employee/agent relationship. The first is the normal one that both manager and employees are effort- as well as risk-averse. The manager will want to monitor employees (because his pay or worth depends on it) in an efficient way, creating incentives for operatives to supply effort by means of specific elements in the pay scheme. Risk will be shared in the optimal contract. Again it should be emphasized that the incentives need not be based upon financial performance but might be linked to other proxies of effort; productivity measures and the like. Thus both management and employees would be covered by some sort of bonus scheme, maybe related to different indicators of performance.

The other facet of the relationship is the ability to control subordinates. Most large firms, almost inevitably, have a number of levels in the hierarchy. This can make it difficult for management to exercise control because orders tend to become more distorted as they pass through more layers;

---

[9]One example here would be coalminers living in remote pit villages, compared with pit managers.

90 per cent compliance at each stage in the hierarchy implies less than 50 per cent compliance from one end to the other over seven stages (see Williamson, 1975, ch. 3). The diffusion of one innovation in particular, originating in the United States between the two world wars, appears to have assisted in ameliorating this problem. The innovation has been to abandon the unitary form of organization in favour of the multidivisional (or 'M') form. Briefly, this involves recasting the company into a number of operating divisions which take day-to-day decisions concerning particular product ranges. Strategic decisions are kept separate, and are decided by the chief executive assisted by a small general office staff. Williamson (1975, ch. 8) covers this in more detail. Evidence for the United States and the UK on the hypothesis that efficiency is thereby improved appears fairly clear-cut (see Thompson, 1983 and references cited therein).

How will these factors differ as between the organizational forms we are examining? In principle, the first — incentives — should not be much affected; incentives can be made to exist in both cases. Nevertheless, it is possible that if in the manager—owner contract nexus the manager bears little risk, this may spill over into a lack of control over employees. Moreover, if in practice the employees under some organizational forms are more powerful than those under other regimes (e.g. unions have more representation in nationalized firms), then this may well lead to above-normal earnings/employment conditions, and so higher costs (see McDonald and Solow, 1981). The second factor, the intra-organizational control problem, may differ between regimes because many publicly owned and regulated firms are not easily divisionally organized since the firm essentially operates in only one area, with others a rather small part of activities.[10] But some successfully divisionalized private companies also operate mainly in one product area.

Let us turn to a different aspect of the manager—employee relationship. The employees can be viewed as a principal to the manager as agent. This may, to some, seem novel, but in fact there are extensive symmetries with shareholders. Shareholders invest their capital in the firm, whilst employees invest their human capital. If the firm does badly they can leave, but this will necessitate a loss of human capital assuming they have accumulated some firm-specific skills. If the firm does very badly, they may be forced to leave, and again lose out. Employees are members of the company (see Aoki, 1983) and have something at stake.

So, from their viewpoint, management's job is to use the factors at its disposal to provide returns to the shareholders, but also to provide returns

[10]Thompson (1983) finds that more diversified firms adopt multidivisional or 'M'-form earlier *ceteris paribus*.

to employees. The employees use the manager as an agent in gaining employment opportunities, signing an 'implicit contract' with the manager.[11] Implicit contract theory suggests that if the agent is risk-neutral, he or she takes all the risk. Employees are therefore paid a fixed wage whatever the state of the world, boom or slump, and, at least in some models, compensated for being laid off, up to the point that they are indifferent between working and not. On the other hand, if both agent and employees are risk-averse, there is risk-sharing: employees' wages vary, being greater in good times.

Consider the position of a risk-averse agent. The agent may be better off claiming times are bad when they are not, if wages are thereby greatly reduced compared to employment and output, so raising the firm's net earnings and the agent's earnings. Moreover, the agent is in a better position to know this than, at least, production workers. Hence there is an adverse selection (or hidden knowledge) problem. How can the employees trust their agent to report fairly the state of nature? As a result, some otherwise non-optimal elements may have to be built into the contractual structure, some incentive compatibility constraints.

With the risk-neutral agent this problem disappears. There is no point in making the claim because there are no savings in wages given the nature of the contract we have discussed. Most probably it is in publicly owned concerns that the agent is more nearly risk-neutral, given what has gone before. Hence in such firms this particular problem is less likely to be relevant.

3.5 Concluding remarks

It is fairly clear from the discussion above that there is a potential for both publicly owned and publicly regulated concerns to perform less efficiently than public liability companies. This is so because the former quite possibly face weaker external constraints and because management may not encounter such sophisticated incentive structures. There are possible offsetting arguments concerning internal structure, but these are in any case not unambiguous in their directional effect. Nevertheless, it is only a potential. More importantly, there are constraints specific to the public sector and to regulated firms, as discussed in the next two chapters, which may improve their efficiency. Therefore we cannot make the a priori assertion that private ownership and unfettered operation is always more efficient. Indeed it would

---

[11]There are parallels here with the rather different 'double moral hazard' problem considered by Cooper and Ross (1985).

be surprising were we able to do so, since there are some fairly clear empirical examples of industries where publicly owned concerns have been of superior or equal efficiency to private ones, as we shall see in chapter 7.

It is not clear how market structure influences the comparison between institutions. One argument (see Caves and Christensen, 1980) is that in competitive industries, all concerns have to be of roughly equal efficiency, whereas in the absence of competition, publicly owned concerns will be inferior. In opposition to this, Kay and Silberston (1984) argue that competition would not necessarily lead to equal efficiency, since publicly owned concerns have the deep purse of public funds on which to draw. In addition they argue that the absence of external yardsticks under monopoly means that no clear tendency is likely here. Again, this seems an empirical question, and it is raised again in chapter 7.

Finally, throughout this chapter we have focused on constraints. Constraints are not sufficient, though. In the textbook theory of the firm, the cost function is drawn assuming both technical and economic efficiency. But this simply shows the best way of producing any particular output at given factor prices; it does not say what output to produce. In order to do that, the firm has to be endowed with an objective, in the textbook firm case, profit maximization.

Thus it is not enough, upon asking the chairman of a state-owned or regulated firm what his objective is, to receive the answer 'To run an efficient business'. The supplementary is, 'How do you decide how large that business should be?'. This brings us straight back to the earlier output comparisons in chapter 2. Left to itself, such a concern may adopt a senseless or ambiguous objective (like, reportedly, London Transport Executive's one-time objective of maximizing passenger miles travelled). Those in charge need to impose some objective, explicitly or implicitly (for example, by imposing a breakeven constraint) in order for the size of the business to be determined.

Notes on the literature

The principal–agent approach to the analysis of firm behaviour is laid out in Strong and Waterson (1987), and the basic theoretical results of agency theory are discussed in Arrow (1984) and Shavell (1979). See also Stiglitz (1985) on this question. Kay and Thompson (1986) apply the analysis to state ownership and privatization. Although it is difficult to get hold of, Lambert and Larcker (1985) is a useful source on executive compensation. McGuinness (1987) contains a useful brief analysis of internal organizational questions, from which other sources can be referenced if required.

Appendix: The Effect of Cost Reductions on Welfare

In section 1.4, we considered an example that illustrated the large potential welfare improvements which price reductions can create. Thus one important target for a regulatory agency is to bring prices closely into line with costs. But costs are not exogenously given, and more efficient firms will have lower costs, other things being equal. Moreover, the analysis of this chapter suggests that efficiency is likely to differ under different regulatory regimes. Hence another important target for the agency (or equally for profit recipients) is to keep the firm's costs under control. In itself, this can have a socially beneficial effect on price (though it need not). As a consequence, it may be that efforts to secure cost reductions actually produce greater benefits than direct price reductions of equivalent size.

Before demonstrating this point directly, we should consider how cost reductions can arise, because different possibilities have different welfare effects. First, let us assume fixed proportions in production. Reductions in factor prices do not then engender changing factor proportions, but of course they do reduce costs. For example, suppose that airline pilots are paid far more than their transfer earnings, but that it always takes three pilots (pilot equivalents) to fly a plane. Reducing their earnings lowers the airline's cost curves and therefore will most likely cause the airline to reduce its prices.

A simple example of a monopoly airline is shown in figure 3.2, in which constant average costs are assumed for simplicity. We assume price is reduced from p_1 to p_2 as a result of a cost reduction from AC_1 to AC_2. Consumers have gained consumer surplus through this price reduction, part of which (FEJN) is a transfer from firm to consumers, the other part being the area labelled FNK. Profits also have increased, from EFGH to JKLM. But part of this increase is a transfer from pilots to the firm, as a result of the lower costs, namely the cross-hatched area HGQM. This obviously cannot be counted as a social welfare gain (or loss). In fact, adding up the various amounts, the social welfare gain is the shaded area FQLK in total.

On the other hand, a reduction in costs can come about through elimination of waste. For example, an input may be priced at above marginal cost in a situation where there are variable proportions in production. With other inputs being priced at marginal cost, this will lead the purchaser to economize on the input in question, compared with its true resource cost, using more of the relatively cheap inputs. But in fact it would be beneficial to all parties for the supplier to receive a lump sum in exchange for the input being priced at marginal cost, because this would lead to optimal

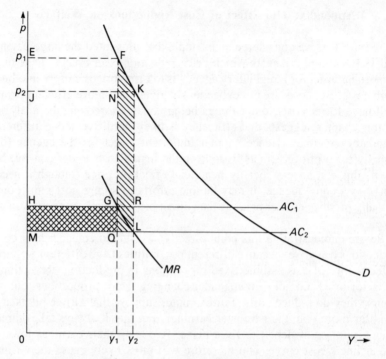

Figure 3.2   The effect of cost reductions on welfare

proportions being used (Vernon and Graham, 1971, have a demonstration). A more straightforward example is where a technically inefficient process is being used.

In these cases, the reduction in the firm's cost is wholly (or, in the variable proportions example, partially) a social gain. In figure 3.2, suppose the move from AC_1 to AC_2 is represented by increased technical efficiency. Then the cross-hatched area can now be counted as a welfare gain. The difference between total welfare gain in this and the previous case is quite significant, and it illustrates the importance of being clear about the underlying factors.

Now, let us consider the options open to a regulatory agency. Suppose it can secure either an x per cent price reduction or an x per cent cost reduction at equal cost to itself; for which should it aim? Assume for simplicity that the firm was previously unregulated, charging monopoly price, and further that demand has approximately constant elasticity in the relevant region. We have the normal monopoly formula:

$$\frac{p - c_i}{p} = 1/\eta, \text{ or } p_i = \frac{\eta}{\eta - 1} c_i \qquad (3.2)$$

where c_i represents a particular value for marginal and average costs and η the absolute value of demand elasticity, invariant with i.

From (3.2), for any two cost levels c_1 and c_2:

$$\frac{p_1 - p_2}{p_1} = \frac{c_1 - c_2}{c_1}.$$

In other words, a proportionate cost reduction of x ($= (c_1 - c_2)/c_1$) will lead to the same proportionate reduction in price, and so an x per cent cost reduction leads to an x per cent price reduction and therefore to the social benefits of that x per cent price reduction (which are area FGRK). But in addition, if the cost reduction succeeds in eliminating pure waste, the extra gain is area HRLM, and even if the cost reduction involves a pure transfer, there is still a small gain of GRLQ. Therefore, since the cost reduction has the same effect as the price reduction but has other effects in addition, it is more worthwhile to strive after, if it is equally easy to obtain.[12] Of course, it may be the case that monitoring of costs compared to an ideal is in practice very much more difficult than monitoring prices relating to costs.

Finally, if different underlying forms of firm differ in efficiency and so in cost, this is obviously of some importance. The analysis above indicates that getting the underlying structure right (i.e. having an efficient firm organization) is at least as important as having control over the firm's prices directly. Indeed, holding prices down to an inefficient level of costs may be inferior in its effects to a form of control in which prices are high but costs are low. This therefore provides a rationale for examining whether and why firm organizations might differ in efficiency, through examining constraints on the organization.

---

[12]It should be noted that the assumption of constant elasticity is important for this simple result to hold.

4

State Control and its Enforcement

Earlier chapters have developed the underlying theory of pricing, efficient industry structure and internal efficiency of the firm. The next stage is to examine in some detail specific institutional cases of types of control. Let us start with the case that probably involves the heaviest hand on the controls, that is, state ownership.

In essence, the objective of a state-controlled natural monopoly could be seen as the maximization of social welfare emanating from the product in question. This social welfare might plausibly, in turn, be identified with the sum of consumer, producer and factor returns. If so, and since any rise in factor prices above alternative use values or any rise in price above marginal cost causes a potential deadweight loss, the most obvious solution is for a price fixed at the level of marginal cost. (An equally acceptable alternative, on the stated criterion, would be perfect price discrimination practised on all consumers down to those willing to pay marginal cost.)

Putting it algebraically, the management's problem is:

$$
\begin{aligned}
\text{Maximize } W &= \int_0^{y_0} p \cdot dy - wx_1 - rx_2 \\
x_1, x_2 &
\end{aligned}
$$

subject to:

$$
\left.
\begin{aligned}
p &= p(y) \\
y &= y(x_1, x_2) \\
w &= w_c \\
r &= r_c
\end{aligned}
\right\}
\tag{4.1}
$$

where W is social benefit as defined above and for simplicity we have assumed two inputs only, say labour and capital. The constraints ensure that the demand curve $p(y)$ is correctly identified, that the firm is producing on its production function $y = y(x_1, x_2)$ and that factors are priced at their alternative use values w_c and r_c. Thus the solution involves technical and economic efficiency in production (being on an isoquant and at the correct point on it), sales or management efficiency in identifying the correct demand curve, and allocative efficiency in choosing the correct output, y_0, that where price equals marginal cost. Since this involves choosing the correct input levels from the desired isoquant, the maximization problem is written with labour and capital as the control variables. It goes without saying that stating the problem is not the same thing as solving it in practice!

Equation (4.1) involves an objective (social welfare maximization in the sense outlined) and several constraints. In the very different world of perfect competition, the constraints are assumed satisfied given competition between firms as to who is to produce, price-taking behaviour and, lastly, the indirect result that the individual profit maximizing behaviour which would be expected from self-seeking entrepreneurs leads to social welfare maximization — the 'invisible hand' result. Here, it is a different matter; neither the objective nor the constraints arise automatically. It is only in the unlikely circumstance that the product market is perfectly contestable *and* that the factor markets are perfectly competitive, that we can be confident of extending the compass of the invisible hand result.

All the foregoing holds true if the state does not own the business in question but simply takes responsibility for its social return. Here the business is regulated. In that case also, the state in principle sets management an objective and imposes constraints so as to achieve the result. However, it may be that management has its own objective, or is forced into one by its shareholders, so that the state may find it needs to impose additional constraints to mould that objective to its own desires.

Of course, we have been discussing the problem in a very abstract manner, in both the state-owned and the state-regulated cases. In practice, the state or its regulatory authority is unlikely to know as much as those in the firm about the demand curve, the production function or, even, the competitive level of factor prices. Therefore, in order to maintain control it cannot specify the production function and so on explicitly as a constraint. It must tackle the problem indirectly, imposing controls which (if they are designed correctly) have an effect equivalent to the constraints in (4.1).

Because there are differences in objectives between state-owned and state-regulated concerns, and also because the actual objectives and constraints have evolved in different ways, the two cases will be discussed in separate chapters. We will confine ourselves here to the state-owned case, leaving regulation to chapter 5.

The framework of the chapter is as follows. We first provide a positive rationale for considering state ownership, by examining its advantages. Then in section 4.2 we consider the question of how prices should be set, focusing first upon the historically important marginal cost doctrine. Section 4.3 examines economists' *models* of constraints and objectives as practised in state-owned firms, whereas section 4.4 looks at the controls imposed in the UK and provides some general remarks on comparisons between these and the economists' suggestions.

4.1 Reasons for state ownership

As we saw in chapter 3, there are fewer 'natural' controls on state-owned than on state-regulated concerns. Therefore, all other things being equal, it would appear that more, or more extensive, controls would have to be placed on state-owned concerns than on regulated ones. However, there are reasons why the state may prefer to own rather than merely to regulate.

The most obvious political reason for state ownership is to ensure social ownership of production, in the particular sense of 'for the people'. Equally obviously this constitutes no reason at all if one does not hold this particular feature in high regard. Nevertheless, there are other political and economic arguments for it.

One frequent argument for state control is that it facilitates economic planning of key sectors of the economy. To take a possible example, state ownership of coal, oil exploration, and gas and electricity industries may facilitate the planning of the energy sector. Other industries can also be influenced, and their arrangements facilitated. For example, the location of an aluminium smelter adjacent to a power station which is in turn adjacent to a coal mine (and a source of cooling water) seems logical but might be very much more difficult to arrange with three completely independent parties to the bargain than if the government and the smelter company alone are involved.

However, the link between planning and state ownership should not be overstated: all companies of any size plan. (Thus, incidentally, planning cannot be equated with socialism.) Therefore planning and the market mechanism are not alternative but are complementary. A government can influence private company plans in a variety of ways, and thus achieve objectives which are essentially the same as those that could be reached by ownership. The activities of the Japanese ministry of International Trade and Industry (MITI) provide an important counter-example to the proposition that planning *requires* extensive state ownership.

A third argument for state control is that it facilitates income redistributional measures. In particular, it may be considered desirable to have universal access to basic utilities and essential services. The standard economist's viewpoint on this is one of suspicion — leave the firms and consumers to themselves and make any necessary corrections to income distribution through appropriate transfers. As has already been pointed out in section 1.2, practical redistributional measures are not costless, so that it is in all probability more efficient to tell the telephone company it has to bear the expense of maintaining rural telephone boxes than to fund these separately. Equally, it may be socially desirable to enforce partial abatement of the fixed charge element for small users of electricity or gas rather than having to identify a more specific form of assistance. Indeed, multiproduct companies will normally have a variety of means open to them for breaking even on their operation, some of which may be approximately equally efficient, so that governmental intervention to choose one amongst them, something facilitated by state ownership, is not necessarily inefficient.

In addition, if the industry concerned creates externalities, these may be dealt with more directly if it is state-owned. Leading on from this, a more general point is that where the objective of the operation is rather broader than profit maximization, shareholder control is probably far less appropriate than state control (see, for example, Baumol, 1984).

Finally, there is the distributional argument that in a state-owned firm there is less clearly an adversarial 'us against them' contest between management and employees, because the profits (if there are any) do not accrue specifically to owners of capital.

In sum, this brief discussion has demonstrated that there are positive reasons for state ownership and control; it is not self-evidently an inferior alternative to state regulation. Having made this point, we can move on to examine the objectives and constraints associated with such enterprises.

4.2 Marginal cost pricing and other objectives

Most of the literature in the area of state control has assumed that marginal cost pricing (with marginal cost at efficient levels) is the objective. There are two qualifications made to this view. First, there has been extensive discussion as to what is or should be meant by 'marginal cost'. In particular, there is the question of short- versus long-run marginal cost, and of marginal cost differing over (say) times of day. Secondly, as is well known, if average cost is still falling at the relevant output, marginal cost pricing leads to deficits. The question then arises as to how these should be funded. We will consider these questions below before moving on to controls in sections 4.3 and 4.4.

First, we may note that the rationale for marginal cost pricing in public enterprises is based upon a Paretian decision-maker operating in an otherwise first-best economy. If all sectors other than the state sector are competitive, the prices in that sector should equal marginal cost. Of course this qualification is unlikely to hold, and indeed it is also unlikely that prices differing from marginal costs in various other sectors are easily correctable. The general theory of the second best then provides the unhelpful result that it is not necessarily better to move prices in those sectors which

66   *State Control and its Enforcement*

can easily be adjusted, so as to align more closely with marginal cost. Nevertheless, it may also be shown that, if the state sector is independent of
the other sectors in consumption and production, then marginal cost pricing should still be pursued. More generally, optimal prices should be based
upon marginal cost and also on demand factors (see e.g. Hagen, 1979),
but the relevant formulae for optimal departures from marginal cost are
rather complex. We will make the (questionable?) assumption that in most
other areas prices do not deviate too far from marginal cost, in which case
marginal cost in this sector is a relevant ideal. Furthermore, we will assume
that the sector to which we are referring accounts for a sufficiently small
part of consumer expenditure that income effects are unimportant. The
benefit of this assumption (Willig, 1976) is that we may use consumer
surplus, the area under the demand curve, as a measure of social benefit.[1]
Any policy that improves (reduces) consumer plus producer surplus then
improves (reduces) social welfare. In other words, we may continue with
a partial equilibrium framework.

Having made assumptions sufficient to ensure that marginal cost is a
desirable objective, we have the question of 'which' marginal cost is relevant. Here, though there has been an extensive debate on the practice concerning long run versus short run, economic theory is essentially clear cut.
There are two aspects to the firm's decision-making: what price to set now,
with given resources, and what price to plan for, in deciding upon investments. The answer can be encompassed within the single principle that
the relevant marginal cost is that concerned with varying output in the relevant period. Supposing, for simplicity, we are concerned only with two
years, price this year should be determined by short-run marginal cost (a
view not endorsed by the 1967 White Paper — see section 4.4), but investment plans for next year should be evaluated (using net present value
methods) based upon long-run marginal costs.

Figure 4.1 illustrates the principle. Assume that the relevant long-run
marginal cost curve remains at LMC throughout. Planned output for this
period was y_1^p, but in practice demand turned out to be given by D_1. The
resulting price and output combination for this period (1) is (p_1, y_1) —
price is set equal to short-run marginal cost SMC_1 and, it turns out in
figure 4.1, is less than long-run marginal cost. In making decisions about
year 2, it is conjectured that demand will have risen to D_2^p. Hence investment plans should be based upon an output of y_2^p selling at p_2^p. If demand
turns out higher in period 2 (e.g. at D_2'), then the actual price would be

---

[1]In the context of the example of section 1.4, the gas industry is almost certainly sufficiently small in Willig's terms to make consumer surplus a very good approximation to
the true benefit to consumers.

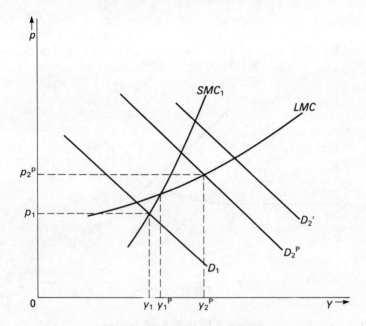

Figure 4.1 Planned and actual price–output combinations

above p_2^p, at the point where D_2' meets SMC_2 (not drawn, to avoid cluttering the figure).

The principle may also be extended to cover cases such as the peak load problem where, because plant is reaching its capacity, marginal costs rise very sharply once a given output has been reached. The short-run decision of a firm running such a plant (e.g. an electricity generating station) is illustrated in figure 4.2. Daytime demand is at level D_D whilst night-time demand is at level D_N. As the figure is drawn, the price p_D charged during the day includes some element of these capacity costs, whereas night-time price only covers running costs.

Such a marginal cost pricing policy would fail to cover total costs if, on average, the prices were below average costs. This is inevitable with a declining-cost technology and correctly anticipated outcomes. There are two obvious solutions. First, any deficit could be underwritten from public funds. Alternatively, the prices could be adjusted somehow so that they met total costs.

If it were decided to impose a breakeven constraint, and assuming that there is more than one product price involved, the target may be achieved in many ways. Confining ourselves for the moment to pricing structures

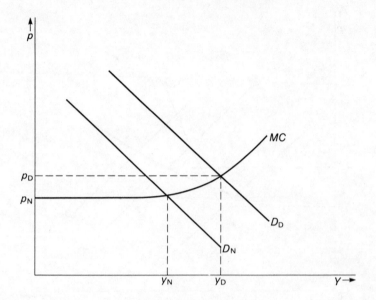

Figure 4.2 Peak load pricing

involving a constant per unit price, we found in section 2.2 that the socially optimal solution is not to raise all prices an equal proportion above average costs, but rather to practice *Ramsey-optimal* (value-based) pricing. Here, in straightforward applications, no price is below its relevant marginal cost and the discrepancy between price and marginal cost is larger, the less elastic is demand for that product (Phillips, 1980).

However, there is no particular reason to confine ourselves to constant per unit prices, and we should also consider *nonlinear outlay schedules*, in which charges are not strictly proportional to the number of units purchased. One example we have already mentioned is perfect price discrimination, in which every consumer pays the maximum they are willing to pay as represented by their position on the market demand curve. But this is essentially of theoretical interest only, and there are far more practical examples.

A commonly proposed and reasonably workable alternative to constant per unit prices is the *two-part tariff* structure. This involves a per unit price below average cost, plus a lump sum fee for the right to consume, which is of sufficient size to ensure at least breakeven. Such tariff structures are widely used (consider, for example, telephone charges) and can in principle lead to outcomes superior to straightforward average cost pricing.

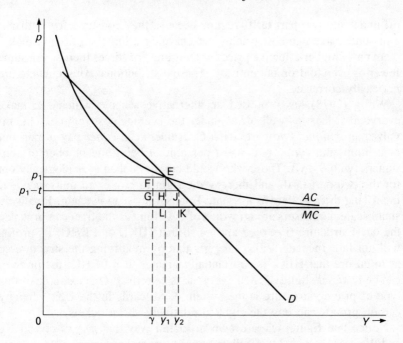

Figure 4.3   Two-part tariff structures

To illustrate, let us revert to the one-product firm, and consider the case represented by figure 4.3. Suppose first that average cost pricing is practised — price is p_1 and quantity y_1. Suppose further that at this price *every* consumer buys x units. Now, the unit price is dropped to $p_1 - t$ and a lump sum fee of tx is charged to everyone who buys the good. No consumer is worse off, because buying x units results in the same total outlay. However, the marginal price of extra units falls to $p_1 - t$, so that some consumers will buy more than x and will gain consumer surplus if their marginal valuation lies between p_1 and $(p_1 - t)$. Hence, total sales increase to y_2, consumers as a group are better off and, since we have $(p_1 - t) \geq c$, so is the firm.

Unfortunately, the situation just described where each consumer takes x units is unlikely. If the good is a normal one, for example, consumers on higher incomes will buy more units than those on low incomes, all other things equal. It remains true (as Ng and Weisser, 1974, show) that a two-part tariff with a non-negative licence fee is socially preferable to a uniform price system in the sense that the welfare of the group is improved. However, some consumers, and these will be the poorer ones, will be worse off under the two-part tariff regime because they consume fewer than x units under average cost pricing, so charging a lump sum fee tx makes them pay a higher effective price for their units or forces them to consume fewer or even to drop out entirely. These distributional consequences are not easily corrected.

Willig (1978) has proposed an alternative scheme which can make everyone at least as well off as under the average cost regime. This involves an *optional* two-part tariff. Consumers can *either* pay p_1 per unit or a lump sum $(\gamma t/n)$ plus $p_1 - t$ per unit, n being the number of consumers (with $\gamma < y_1$). Those who would buy more than (γ/n) logically opt for the two-part tariff and thereby the right to buy extra units at $p_1 - t$, improving their welfare as a result. Total sales rise to y_2 again. Relatively small scale purchasers are no worse off. As long as the firm can organize the tariff structure (i.e. p_1, t and γ) so that HJKL $\geq$ FEHG, its profits will not fall. Indeed, Willig suggests that by modifying the structure so as to ensure that HJKL is substantially greater than FEHG, the price p_1 can be lowered slightly. Then everyone is better off. One example of this type of pricing structure is the system of railcards in the UK, whereby certain groups can buy the right to relatively cheap tickets.[2]

Notice that figure 4.3 is drawn in such a way that $p_1 - t > c$, and Ng and Weisser show that this will be socially optimal as long as average consumption exceeds marginal consumption, the normal case. In Willig's example also, it is necessary for the workings of the scheme that marginal price exceeds marginal cost (so that HJKL > 0). However, Willig further demonstrates that two-part tariffs of his sort are often dominated by more complex schedules in which the largest purchaser pays a marginal price equal to marginal cost. One example of a more complex schedule is a 'declining block' tariff (Leland and Meyer, 1976).

Returning to our main theme, the practical choice of pricing systems in increasing returns cases lies between deficit financing, Ramsey-optimal pricing, two-part tariffs, declining block tariffs, or some other non-uniform pricing scheme. If lump sum taxes are straightforward to levy and cheap to administer, the first course is the best. However, most taxes which are a practical proposition create their own distortions in the economy and involve non-trivial collection costs. In this case, there is a tradeoff between distortions induced by a subsidy policy and distortions induced by some prices being above marginal cost. Models in the following section tend to assume breakeven along with uniform pricing.

---

[2]Of course the purpose of these is also to discriminate against certain classes of passenger who cannot use them, e.g. business people.

4.3 Modelling the constraints and objectives

As was said in the introductory section, it is not feasible for the government to direct the firm to produce specific quantities at specific prices because the government necessarily knows less than the firm about underlying demand and cost conditions. Instead, indirect constraints are used. In order to investigate the operation of such constraints, we will first look at some theoretical models which cast light on the various problems involved in the government—management 'game', before turning to the next section to consider some features of the control structure in the UK, so as to see some practical illustrations of the points.

Altruistic manager models

Gravelle (1977 and elsewhere) and others have formulated the general problem of a public firm subject to a rate of return constraint, as follows:

$$\underset{Y,X}{\text{Max}} \; S(Y) \; - \; wx_1 - rx_2 \; \text{subject to:} \; f(Y,X) \; \geq \; 0$$
$$R(Y) - wx_1 - (r+\pi)x_2 \; \geq \; 0 \qquad (4.2)$$

where Y is the firm's output vector, X is the firm's input vector (x_1,x_2), w and r are the respective (fixed) factor prices equivalent to their social costs, $f(Y,X)$ is the production relationship (implicit production function), $S(Y)$ is consumers' willingness to pay (i.e. the integral of the area under the demand curve), $R(Y)$ is revenue and $r+\pi$ is the required rate of return. To put it in words, the manager is in effect altruistic, wishing to maximize the difference between social benefits and costs. However, management is constrained in this not only by the technical capabilities, but also by the requirement to break even on the basis of rate of return above the norm.

Assuming binding constraints, and taking the case where there is only one product y with price p (or independent demands), means we may write the Lagrangean function from (4.2) with multipliers μ and λ as:

$$L = S(y) \; - \; wx_1 - rx_2 \; + \; \mu f(y,X) \; + \; \lambda[py \; - \; wx_1 \; - \; (r+\pi)x_2]$$

Then, the first order conditions give:

$$p + \mu f' + \lambda(p + yp') = 0 \qquad (4.3)$$
$$-w(1 + \lambda) + \mu f_1 \qquad = 0 \qquad (4.4)$$
$$-r(1 + \lambda) + \mu f_2 - \lambda\pi = 0 \qquad (4.5)$$

f_i being $\partial f/\partial x_i$, f' being $\partial f/\partial y$, and $S'(y) \equiv p$. Hence from (4.3), (4.4):

$$p(1 + \lambda) + \lambda y\, p' + \frac{f'}{f_1}\, w(1 + \lambda) = 0$$

But $-wf'/f_1 = C_1$, the marginal cost of production when x_2 is given, since $-f_1/f'$ is the marginal product of x_1. Rearranging:

$$\frac{p - C_1}{p} = \frac{\lambda}{1 + \lambda} \frac{1}{\eta} \tag{4.6}$$

where η is the elasticity of demand, written as a positive number (i.e. $-p/yp'$).

A similar series of manipulations using (4.3) and (4.5) yields:

$$\frac{p - C_2}{p} = \frac{\lambda}{1 + \lambda} \left[\frac{1}{\eta} + \frac{\pi x_2}{py} E_2 \right] \tag{4.7}$$

where $E_2 = (\partial x_2/\partial y) \cdot y/x_2$, the elasticity of capital with respect to output. Notice that if $\pi = 0$, this collapses to the equivalent expression for the labour input. However, with $\pi > 0$, since the second term in the bracket is positive, $(p - C_2)/p > (p - C_1)/p$. Therefore $C_2 < C_1$, so that rewriting in terms of marginal products:

$$\frac{MP_2}{MP_1} > \frac{r}{w};$$

in other words the capital to labour ratio is not what would be optimal given factor prices — capital is employed to a lesser extent and labour to a greater extent than is desirable. This is a variant of the 'Averch – Johnson effect' for regulated firms which is discussed in chapter 5 below.

The distortion in factor usage compared with factor prices and social costs implies that marginal costs are higher than they should be. This is illustrated in figure 4.4, which represents a given level of output on iso-quant $\bar{y}$. The market factor price ratio suggests A as the appropriate combination but, because the return on capital required is above normal, combination B is chosen. As a consequence, valuing the inputs at their true factor prices indicates higher costs of producing that output (dashed isocost line) than need be. Nevertheless, Gravelle (1981b) shows, after some considerable manipulation, that, given the distortion p, the optimal price for the product is at marginal cost.

As we can see from (4.6) and (4.7), prices are above marginal costs. In fact, if we were to set $\pi = 0$, the price cost margins would be exactly equivalent to those obtained from the Ramsey optimal pricing problem, precisely because the problem would then be an example of the Ramsey problem.

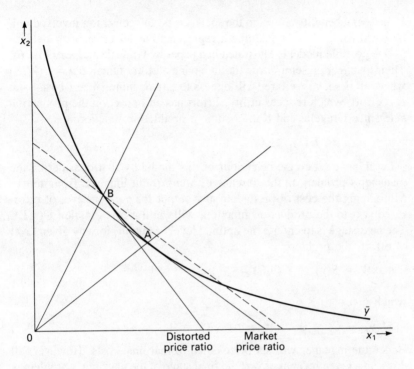

Figure 4.4 The effects of factor price distortions

In this model then, there are two distortions. First, marginal costs are unnecessarily high. Secondly, prices are high compared with marginal costs. The second comes about because of the breakeven requirement and is necessary if subsidies are disallowed. The first comes from the artificially high return on capital. It is an unnecessary constraint, since without it the manager would do better. This is surely a general result, that if the management left to itself would act in a socially optimal way along the lines represented in (4.1), it is fatuous, indeed counterproductive, to constrain it.

Managerial utility models

Unfortunately, it would be unwise to expect managers of publicly owned firms to act in the selfless way modelled above. We need to consider more carefully what they might have as their objectives. Then, if their maximand is not solely social welfare maximization, there is room for constraints to have an influence for the good. We have seen that constraints can introduce distortions, but we will also find that they can improve performance.

If the social benefits outweigh the social costs, the constraint involved will be worthwhile. Let us examine a representative selection of models.

One possible model is illustrated in a paper by Gravelle and Katz (1976). Their manager is 'semi-altruistic' in having a utility function $u = u(W,E)$ where W is social welfare (willingness to pay S, minus factor costs) and E is effort, which reduces utility. Effort has an impact on the production side since Gravelle and Katz assume a production function:

$$y = f(x_1, x_2, E), f_E \geq 0.$$

Let us investigate the behaviour of this model by first considering the manager's problem in the absence of a constraint imposed from above. Minimizing the cost of producing any output for a given level of effort E, subject to the production function, will yield a cost function $C(y,E)$. The next stage is to choose the optimal level of output, for any given level of effort, the problem:

$$\max_y W = S(y) - C(y,E)$$

which gives

$$S'(y) - C_y = 0 \quad \text{or} \quad p - C_y = 0 \qquad (4.8)$$

Hence the manager will set price equal to marginal costs. However, all this is at a given level of effort; the final stage of the manager's problem is

$$\max_E u(W,E)$$

and

$$\frac{du}{dE} = u_w \frac{\partial W}{\partial E} + u_E = u_w \left[\frac{\partial W}{\partial y} \cdot \frac{\partial y}{\partial E} + \frac{\partial W}{\partial E} \right] + u_E$$

$$= u_w \left[(p - C_y) \cdot \frac{\partial y}{\partial E} - C_E \right] + u_E.$$

On equating this first-order condition to zero, using result (4.8) that $p = C_y$ we have: $u_w C_E = u_E$, hence $C_E < 0$. Further input of effort would lead to reduced costs at the manager's optimum. Therefore, if the social cost of additional effort is presumed to be zero, a socially insufficient amount of effort is supplied.

In the Gravelle and Katz model then, there is scope for a potential improvement in performance to be induced by constraints on the firm, despite the fact that such constraints can lead to other distortions. They examine the impact of an absolute profit constraint $\pi - t \geq 0$, a percentage markup constraint, $\pi - tc \geq 0$, and a rate of return constraint as before, $\pi - (t-r)x_2 \geq 0$. A necessary (but not sufficient) condition for performance improvements is that they force the manager to lower costs. Unfortunately general results are elusive; it is not the case that any of these constraints will always improve performance, neither is it true that one necessarily dominates another. Even in the simplest case, the lump sum target, it can only be shown that the target can be used to improve welfare under the assumptions that E is neutral in its effect on production and that there are non-decreasing returns to scale.

It may be true that people put themselves forward for managerial posts in public industry because they have a genuine desire to improve social welfare (though they dislike effort). If we changed 'public industry' to 'charitable foundations' then only a complete cynic would discount this motive. Nevertheless, it might be wise also to consider models in which managers are in no way altruistic, to see whether the results are different.

Suppose then that the manager has a utility function of the form $u = u(I,E)$, where I is income and E is effort.[3] Without going into the details of modelling procedure, it is easy to see that there are now two sources of inefficiency rather than one. Because altruism has disappeared, price will no longer be set equal to marginal cost (however defined), as well as marginal cost being, possibly, inefficiently high. Also, certain constraints have the potential to make both problems worse. For example, a return on capital constraint could be met by raising prices above what would have been chosen, as well as by distorting the combinations in which factors are used.

It might be thought that combinations of restraints would help to solve the problem. A plausible combination is suggested by Rees (1968): link managerial rewards to the firm's profit, but impose pricing rules to prevent prices being set monopolistically. Here, it would seem, management concentrates on efficiency as the only way to improve pay. However, in his (admittedly slightly more general) model of this problem, Gravelle (1981a) shows that the intuitive argument is misleading; extra effort can actually reduce profit.

Nevertheless, this suggestion by Rees does contain one useful pointer: if managers are non-altruistic, controls on them must influence their pay in order to affect performance. Additionally, assuming we are interested

---

[3] An alternative employed by Gravelle (1981a) has $u=u(p,I,E)$ — since the manager consumes the product, he has an interest in its price. We think this less plausible as a formulation since (*a*) usually the product will be a very small part of his income, (*b*) sometimes (e.g. with rail travel) it is actually supplied free. This is not to deny there may be indirect effects induced by high prices, but that is not what is being modelled.

in social welfare, the manager's pay should be made a function of that, if possible. Yet social welfare would seem impossible to measure, so it seems we reach an impasse.

It is here that the ingenious suggestion of Finsinger and Vogelsang (1981) comes in, to provide what might be called an almost ideal constraint. They propose that a bonus be paid which is based upon an approximation to the *change* in social welfare.[4] Specifically, the 'incentive component' of the managerial emolument package that they propose for period t is given by a function of the increase in profits and the decrease in price between period $t-1$ and period t:

$$I_t = (\Pi_t - \Pi_{t-1}) + y_{t-1}(p_{t-1} - p_t). \tag{4.9}$$

Assuming for the moment that the cost curve $C_{t-1}(y)$ does not change between periods, we can write this:

$$I_t = (y_t - y_{t-1})p_t - [C_{t-1}(y_t) - C_{t-1}(y_{t-1})].$$

Such an area is represented in figure 4.5 by the shaded portion, as can be seen by noting that the first term represents the rectangle ABCD and the second, the area under the marginal cost curve $C'_{t-1}(y)$ between y_{t-1} and y_t (i.e. the integral $\int_{y_{t-1}}^{y_t} C'_{t-1}(y) \cdot dy$).

To see the beneficial effect of Finsinger and Vogelsang's constraint, consider the position of a manager coming in to control an industry in which price is substantially above marginal cost. The way to earn a bonus is to reduce price. Subsequent reductions in price will attract bonuses in subsequent periods, until price is driven to equality with marginal cost; a bonus is paid only if there is a change in price and (or) output. Thus, the bonus encourages movement of price towards the level of marginal cost. Moreover, the bonus is in fact a first order approximation to the true change in welfare, which in figure 4.5 is the shaded area plus the dotted area ABE. Hence the manager increases income by earning the incentive payment, but social welfare is also increased thereby, this to a greater extent, and permanently.

The real merit in this suggestion is that it is based upon (in principle) easily observed magnitudes — those calculating the bonus need know only about price, output and cost levels in each period; they do not need to estimate either demand or cost functions. Therefore it seems there is an easy, cheap and extremely efficient method for rewarding managers in such a way as to elicit efficient performance.

---

[4]An earlier suggestion by Loeb and Magat (1979) to pay a bonus based upon the level of consumer surplus falls foul of the political problem that to pay all the social benefits to an individual is infeasible in practice.

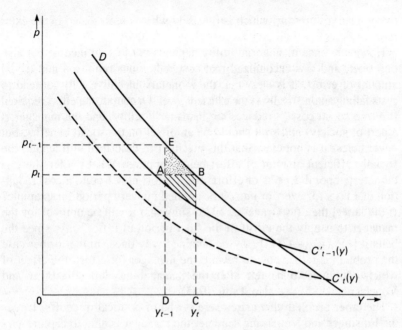

Figure 4.5 Incentive schemes and managerial effort

Unfortunately, there are problems. Gravelle (1985) points to an implicit assumption which, when relaxed, gives rise to one of them: 'that either no managerial effort is required to reduce costs or that such effort does not yield disutility to managers' (p. 115). To see the impact of relaxing this, we return to equation (4.9), but this time allow the cost curve to be pushed downwards by managerial effort in controlling costs between periods $t-1$ and t. We then have

$$I_t = (y_t - y_{t-1})p_t - [C_{t-1}(y_t) - C_{t-1}(y_{t-1})] + [C_{t-1}(y_t) - C_t(y_t)].$$

The extra final term shows that the incentive structure does indeed reward managerial effort in reducing costs. Moreover, the reward is in line with the improvement in social welfare since the total improvement in welfare is the area between the demand curve and $C_t'(y)$ (the dashed curve in figure 4.5) up to y_t minus the area between demand and $C_{t-1}'(y)$ up to y_{t-1}. The extra bit not captured in the previous case is the area between the two curves up to y_t, which is precisely what is represented in the extra term.

However, once managerial utility depends not just on income but also on effort, and it is recognized that cost reductions require a non-trivial amount of effort, it is clear that the monetary incentive will not lead to costs falling automatically to the efficient level. Of course, the effort required is a true social cost (it reduces the manager's utility, and the manager is a part of society) and so it should be an offset on the social benefits, but nevertheless it is not clear that this mechanism described will lead to the socially efficient amount of effort being supplied. What matters here is the intertemporal aspects of effort. Does effort now lead to a cost reduction that lasts for ever, or must it be applied in every period for example? If the latter, then (as Gravelle, 1985, suggests) it will be optimal for the manager to supply the effort in the final period of office only, since the benefit $[C_{t-1}(y_t) - C_t(y_t)]$ may be obtained only once. In the former case the problem is rather how to reward the manager for effort, the effect of which continues to be felt after the manager has left (Finsinger and Vogelsang, 1985; see also Tam, 1985).

The other problem that arises here is one of political tradeoffs. Under the Finsinger and Vogelsang scheme, the manager is able to capture virtually all the increase in social benefits for him or herself in the form of a bonus — in other words the social return is very narrowly distributed. This may lead to huge bonuses being paid to the manager. Yet actually, the scheme would still work within their framework if, say, the manager received one tenth of I_t — the incentives would still be in the right direction. However, this result does not carry through in the same way to the cases we have just been discussing where managerial utility depends on effort as well as income. Reducing the fraction of benefits I_t which the manager receives will reduce the amount of effort put in, *ceteris paribus*. The price of keeping the bonus down to manageable proportions is a somewhat less efficient outcome.

These comments should not be allowed to cloud the picture too much. It is fairly clear from the discussion above that, whatever the type of managerial utility function assumed, some controls may be imposed which can improve performance.[5] It is also worth noting that wherever a manager's utility depends partly upon income, a bonus scheme of the Finsinger–Vogelsang type is likely to improve performance, whereas other controls we have discussed (e.g. rate of return on capital) need not improve efficiency.

---

[5]Vogelsang (1986) extends this incentive literature to link with the two-part tariff literature of section 4.2.

4.4 Controls on nationalized industries in the UK

Having provided a theoretical framework of control, we can now examine the types of controls employed, using the UK as an obvious example. Essentially, there are four types of control which have been exercised for some period: first, the 'White Paper' controls on pricing, investment and financial targets; secondly, external financing limits (EFLs) imposed by the Treasury; thirdly, efficiency audits by the Monopolies and Mergers Commission (MMC); and fourthly, direct controls on management itself. The first and second of these may be thought of, roughly, as equivalent to capital market constraints implemented by the stock market and banks; the last as a form of managerial labour market constraint. Here, I will provide a broad overview of each control, then an assessment based upon this overview; more detailed commentaries on aspects of the controls may be found elsewhere (e.g. Heald, 1980; Webb, 1980, on the White Paper controls).

Pricing criteria were first laid down in detail in the 1967 (second) White Paper — prices should be *related* to (long-run) marginal costs, without arbitrary cross-subsidization, but should be sufficient to cover full accounting costs including the opportunity cost of capital. This could be seen as an approximation to a Ramsey-optimal price structure, though the analogy is probably rather forced. The 1978 White Paper modified this by providing for greater flexibility and by linking prices in price-setting industries to the financial target set.

Investment procedures were changed more substantially between these two White Papers. In the 1967 Paper, investment appraisal was to follow the net present value method, with a test discount rate (TDR) set first at 8 per cent, later at 10 per cent. The emphasis was on a yes/no decision regarding new investment, rather than questions of choice of technique. Unfortunately, much of the investment that took place was never evaluated in this way because it was regarded as 'inescapable', that is, necessary to supply a satisfactory service level, rather than the level of service supplied being part of the decision-making procedure. Because of these problems, the 1978 White Paper replaced the TDR by a required rate of return (RRR) procedure.

The RRR is the *ex post* return (5 per cent) which each industry has to use in appraising its capital programme in entirety, taking into account non-revenue-earning items as well as direct revenue earners — this provides the guidelines for the investment programme. In cases of choice between techniques and decisions about when to invest, this rate is also to be used as a test discount rate.

Leaving aside the (many important and detailed) criticisms which people have made of these procedures, it is clear that, in principle, developing a basis for appraising investment projects is of considerable importance. Furthermore, the rate of return to be used in present value calculations should derive from some sort of comparison with the private sector. To this rather limited extent, the methods seem unexceptionable.

Financial targets came in earlier, in the 1961 White Paper. They are normally in the form of a return on net assets, somehow defined, hence they imply a constraint of the type $\Pi/K \geq \pi$, such as we have considered theoretically earlier. Such a target can in principle help in controlling the industry's activities, though we should recall that *if* managers were social welfare maximizing, the constraint would be superfluous. In fact, financial targets might be seen as equivalent to constraints imposed by shareholders in a public company who require dividends of a certain level (or indeed as related to constraints on regulated companies who must earn no *more* than a certain return on capital; see chapter 5).

In very simple models, the RRR can be seen to imply, or be implied by, the financial target, but because of the differing time periods, differing accounting conventions, the nature of existing capital stock, and so on, the relationship is unlikely to be straightforward in practice. Hence it is unlikely that one or the other constraint is truly redundant.

Both these controls must be distinguished from a third, namely external financing limits. These act (in principle, anyway) as a constraint on the difference between borrowing this year and borrowing last year. Hence they are rather like the overdraft limit placed on a private sector customer by its bank. The societal benefits of this are akin to those arising from the imposition of general controls on financial efficiency of the firm — forcing it to think more carefully about its spending. On the other hand, there are costs. Suppose a particular nationalized firm wants to institute a project that has a very favourable rate of return but which involves heavy capital outlays prior to any revenues being generated. Despite meeting both RRR and financial target criteria, the existence of an external financing limit may stop such a project proceeding. A private sector firm in similar circumstances could issue shares to raise money or could persuade the bank to increase the overdraft, but for its own (macroeconomic) reasons, the Treasury may be less amenable. Hence, worthwhile projects may not proceed or may be unnecessarily delayed, and plans may suddenly have to be changed when constraints are tightened (see also Likierman, 1984).

The 1978 White Paper also proposed that the nationalized industries should produce what are sometimes called 'non-financial performance indicators'. These are essentially meant to be measures of productivity and of service quality, and the idea is both that targets be set, and that analysis of outcomes be presented. In principle this seems sensible, since for many of the industries, particularly those with monopoly power, information on financial outcomes is of only limited relevance in indicating the value for money that society enjoys from the industries. However, it is obviously important that the targets are relevant (e.g. based upon international comparisons), that reasonable detail on the outcomes is available, and most importantly that clearly defined action is taken to improve poor performance. Only limited progress in this direction has been made so far. For example, in British Rail's 1984/5 Annual Report, numerous performance indicators are illustrated, mostly demonstrating improved performance, but performance against target is seldom mentioned, and only two international comparisons are given.

An important supplement to these direct and internal controls is provided by efficiency audits. Efficiency audits have no real private sector counterpart since monopoly references, though they also are carried out by the Monopolies and Mergers Commission, are more limited in scope. One major difference is that efficiency audits mix comments on monopoly abuse and performance with a great deal of what might be called management consultancy. They can involve extensive interviews and investigations throughout all levels of the firm's structure, resulting in detailed recommendations concerning management structures, financial controls and so on. For example, efficiency audits have proposed major shake-ups in the boards (e.g. Severn−Trent Water Authority), allocation of new cost and profit centres (e.g. London Transport Executive), greater realism in investment appraisals (e.g. National Coal Board), changes in manpower practices (e.g. the Post Office), modification of pricing practices (e.g. Caledonian MacBrayne), and more use of (financial and non-financial) performance indicators. One of the major weaknesses is, perhaps, a lack of sufficient follow-up on the recommendations. Many of these management activities would occur automatically in best-practice private companies, spurred on by managers adopting broad views of their briefs, although it is not always clear what motivates the manager to behave in this way — perhaps the operation of the managerial labour market?

This brings us to the final and least developed aspect of the controls, namely factors concerning management directly. There are two elements to this, first the composition of nationalized industry boards and secondly the managerial incentive package. Jones and O'Brien (1982) have produced a useful study regarding board composition. Very briefly, they discovered that public sector boards were smaller on average, had more part-time members, had a broader membership background; members had a shorter length of service, held fewer outside appointments and were paid less than private sector boards. In addition, they suffered from time to time through gaps in chairmanship because ministers had failed to appoint in time. Not all of these differences are necessarily for the worse, but the last four mentioned clearly are. If the board is to take important decisions, it should be capable of doing so wisely. Here part-time members could take on a significant role if they were allocated specific monitoring responsibilities and duties, but their current situation and pay militates against that (Henney, 1984).

The incentive package for management similarly differs quite substantially between the public sector and large private sector companies. On the one hand, tenure in top positions is normally limited through a more explicit contractual term of office than is employed in the private sector, and self-perpetuating oligarchies cannot form. On the other hand (at least until very recently), the 'emolument package' consisted simply of a standard salary offer. For example, the 'going rate' in 1980 for the chairmen of the major industries (gas, aerospace, shipbuilding, railways, coal, etc.) was £48,000, at a time when the top executives of BP, ICI and the like were earning between two and three times that amount, including bonuses but without accounting for various fringe benefits. Presumably this influences relative salary structures further down the hierarchy as well. The picture in 1982 shows a similar, though not quite as marked, uniformity in the state sector, and their salaries may move towards greater accord with market conditions.

Whether executive emoluments in the major nationalized industries increasingly move apart from each other or not, one feature they cannot incorporate is a direct stake in the firm itself. In particular, in the private sector, following tax concessions in the 1984 budget, many large companies have introduced executive share option schemes which will provide senior employees with substantial benefits depending upon company performance. Indeed, privatized companies have also introduced them, e.g. British Telecom. The work reported on in section 3.3 suggested that there may be economic efficiency (as well as taxation efficiency) reasons for the introduction of share options, and in general it suggested that managerial emolument packages should not be in the form of a straight salary but should involve some performance-improving subtleties.

This general approach to efficient emolument packages is markedly absent from the reward structures of public sector companies. Moreover, given the disparity in actual salaries, it is unlikely that the more general 'managerial labour market' constraint on operation is fully effective since, as we said in chapter 3, it is likely that the public sector trawls for talent in a different pool, at least in the UK.[6] On the assumption that the people

[6]These things can of course differ from country to country. Arguably, the position in France is rather different (see Perotin and Estrin, 1986).

actually being appointed were (unlike their private sector counterparts) altruistic, this would be no bad thing, but it would be foolish to believe altruism were always the case. There seems no real reason why managerial bonus schemes of the Finsinger and Vogelsang (1981) type cannot be introduced in order to provide incentives to greater efficiency, and in fact these are more relevant than profit-based bonuses given that the firms concerned have monopoly power.

In summary, we see that there is a range of controls on public sector concerns which, in very broad terms, corresponds to the controls on private sector firms. In neither public nor private cases are we assured that they all lead to greater efficiency. In the particular case of public sector firms' management constraints/rewards, it is fairly clear that there is room for improvement.

Notes on the literature

The literature in this area is very extensive and much of it is in book form, so that the list provided here is necessarily selective and omits some important studies. On the subject area generally, Rees (1984) and Curwen (1986) provide good modern approaches, Rees concentrating upon theoretical analysis and Curwen on controls and on privatization (one of the topics of chapter 7). Rees, and also Yarrow (1986), for example, discuss reasons for state ownership. On pricing, Brown and Sibley (1986) provide a very thorough coverage of nonlinear outlay/pricing schedules. An extensive theoretical treatment of issues such as those covered in section 4.3 is Bös (1986), but see in addition the debate between Tan, Finsinger and Vogelsang, and others in the *Quarterly Journal of Economics* for February 1985. Byatt (1984) is one of the best sources on the material of section 4.4. Finally, one area which has not received full justice in our coverage is the extensive empirical tradition of examining industries case by case to develop views on efficiency. Two very useful sources in this area are Pryke (1981) and Harlow (1977).

5

Rate Regulation Schemes and their Enforcement

State ownership, the subject of the previous chapter, might be thought too rigid a form of control over an industry, or too subject to political interference; in some circumstances it might be viewed as ideologically unacceptable. Yet for various reasons some form of long-term control over an industry might be thought desirable. In that case, the obvious alternative is for the firm to be in private hands but subject to a state regulatory body. This solution has proved historically popular in the United States and, in a rather different form, increasingly popular recently in the UK.

The purpose of the regulatory body is to control monopoly power in the industry in question, often also to ensure maintenance of standards, and perhaps to keep 'wasteful' competition at bay. We shall focus on the first of these tasks (where the results are least straightforward). Its purpose, then, is to remove the potential effects of monopoly, most obviously supercompetitive prices and supernormal profits. This is attempted in two main ways: by regulating the rate of return on capital, and by regulating prices directly. The aim is to reduce prices to breakeven levels. Hence we are talking about average rather than marginal cost pricing overall as the normal practical objective, though multipart tariffs, along the lines discussed in section 4.2, will often be superior to uniform price schedules, for example of the Ramsey kind (see Brown and Sibley, 1986).

In section 5.1, models of this process are developed. These are extended in section 5.2 to bring in some complicating features. More practical elements are covered in section 5.3 through the use of examples.

5.1 Models of regulatory constraints

I shall attempt only to cover basic models of the two major types of restraint — rate of return regulation and price regulation — and then to discuss some of the major questions they raise.

The Averch–Johnson model

Suppose a regulated firm wishes to maximize profit, but is subject to the constraint that it must not earn more than a specific rate of return s on its capital, where $r < s < r_m$, r being the cost of capital to this firm and r_m the maximum that would be earned at the unconstrained monopoly point.[1] What effects will this have upon the firm? The Averch–Johnson (A–J) effect (1962) is that the firm becomes 'overcapitalized' and in this sense relatively inefficient, though we will have to be slightly more precise about what happens later on.

Demonstrating the basics of the A–J effect is most straightforwardly done by using the standard Lagrangean technique, although this conceals some important points, to be explained below. The firm maximizes:

$$\Pi = p \cdot y(x_1, x_2) - wx_1 - rx_2 \tag{5.1}$$

subject to the (for simplicity, binding) constraint:

$$\frac{py - wx_1}{x_2} = s \tag{5.2}$$

x_1 and x_2 being inputs of labour and capital respectively. Thus, we have the Lagrangean:

$$L = py(x_1, x_2) - wx_1 - rx_2 - \lambda(py - wx_1 - sx_2) \tag{5.3}$$

from which we obtain the first order conditions:

$$(1 - \lambda)R_1 - (1 - \lambda)w = 0 \tag{5.4}$$
$$(1 - \lambda)R_2 - (1 - \lambda)r = \lambda(r - s) \tag{5.5}$$

where R_i ($i=1,2$) means the marginal revenue product of factor i (i.e., marginal physical product y_i ($\equiv \partial y/\partial x_i$) times the marginal revenue of selling the commodity produced).

Without the constraint, the ratio of the factor prices would equal the ratio of marginal revenue products. This would also equal the ratio of the marginal physical products, since marginal revenue will cancel. Thus, an unconstrained monopolist utilizes factors in the same efficient proportions as (but to a lesser extent than) does a perfectly competitive firm.

---

[1]It may legitimately be queried why $s > r$. There are two aspects to the answer to this question. First, when s is set equal to r, the problem described below becomes indeterminate. Second, on a practical level, if s were set at the average cost of capital to all firms, it would be likely that the cost to an established utility would be below this, because there are relatively few risks associated with running utilities.

In the A−J case, however, dividing (5.5) by (5.4) we obtain:

$$\frac{y_2}{y_1} = \frac{r}{w} - \frac{\lambda}{1-\lambda} \frac{s-r}{w}. \tag{5.6}$$

Now, it can be shown[2] that $0 < \lambda < 1$. Therefore, with $s > r$, equation (5.6) shows that $y_2/y_1 < r/w$. This is the 'overcapitalization' result.

Having stated the result, we should insert an important caveat (Baumol and Klevorick, 1970). The result is that, at the level of output the regulated firm chooses, it opts for a more capital intensive process than would an unregulated firm at that output. It does not mean that the firm will purchase capital equipment which then lies idle. Nor does it necessarily imply anything about either:

(1) the capital−labour ratio relative to that of an unconstrained profit maximizing monopolist; or
(2) the output of the constrained relative to the unconstrained firm.

These latter are important issues.

In particular, a small inefficiency in production might be tolerated if the regulation resulted in a considerable expansion of output from the unconstrained monopoly level which thereby reduced monopoly welfare loss. But does this occur? As a supplementary question, if the regulatory authorities gain skill in deciding s, in the sense of moving it closer to r, will that reduce the extent of overcapitalization? The answer to the main question is that output expansion is likely but not inevitable. The answer to the supplementary, at least in one sense, is in the negative.

I shall not examine either of these points in rigorous detail. To sketch the analysis, differentiating the production function $y = y(x_1, x_2)$ with respect to s we have:

$$\frac{dy}{ds} = y_1 \frac{dx_1}{ds} + y_2 \frac{dx_2}{ds}.$$

We are interested in dx_2/ds, and subsequently, dy/ds. The constraint (5.2) can be written: $R - wx_1 = sx_2$, where R is total revenue. Differentiating totally: $(R_2 - s)dx_2 + (R_1 - w)dx_1 = x_2\, ds$, but then from the first order

---

[2] If the problem had been set up with constraint (5.2) in inequality form as a Kuhn–Tucker problem, and assuming x_1, $x_2 > 0$, then it would transpire that $\lambda \geq 0$. However, we have already seen that $\lambda \neq 0$, since this would be contrary to the assumption that the firm is constrained. In addition, $\lambda \neq 1$, which, incidentally legitimizes the division of (5.5) by (5.4) to obtain (5.6), for else L in (5.3) collapses to the illegitimate $r = s$. Moreover, the second order conditions imply $\lambda < 1$ (Baumol and Klevorick, 1970). In summary, $0 < \lambda < 1$.

condition (5.4), $R_1 - w = 0$, and from (5.5), $R_2 = (r - \lambda s)/(1 - \lambda)$ after rearrangement. Hence:

$$\frac{dx_2}{ds} = \frac{x_2}{R_2 - s} = \frac{(1 - \lambda)x_2}{r - s} < 0.$$

This says that as s falls towards r, the absolute amount of capital employed rises. Setting an allowed rate of return s closer to the true cost of capital will not reduce the *absolute* capital bias and hence need not reduce the relative capital intensity of the regulated firm — this obviously depends upon how the labour input responds.

Moving to the main question, output increases as a result of a reduction in s below r_m when $dy/ds < 0$. This result is guaranteed if, as is normal, capital and labour are complements in production, but it would not be true if the negative impact of dx_2/ds were outweighed by a positive dx_1/ds.

The point of this digression is not to note a curiosum. Rather by showing that an output increase is not the automatic result of imposing the return on capital constraint, it illustrates clearly that the extent to which output increases is clearly dependent upon the form of the production function involved.

Assuming there is an increase in output, a tradeoff exists between the socially desirable effect of this increased output and the socially wasteful distortion in factor proportions. This tradeoff is illustrated in figure 5.1.[3] As we discussed in section 4.3, input combination distortions induce higher costs, which in the present context are illustrated by regulation resulting in marginal cost curve MC_R rather than MC. The increase in output resulting from regulation is $y_R - y$. Hence the social gain from regulation is area AFGH whilst the cost is BCEF.

Having described the basic Averch–Johnson framework, I could go on to pursue the vast literature on its ramifications. I choose not to do this in more than a very limited way, because our main focus is on comparison between schemes. The next few paragraphs discuss two of the most important qualifications that have been explored analytically and concludes with some points of general relevance to regulatory schemes.

As we shall see in section 5.3, the rate-making process is not as straightforward as that laid out in the A–J model. One early modification made to the analytics was to consider the effects of 'regulatory lag' — that is, the fact that rates are not continually adjusted but are revised from time to time with a delay.

---

[3]For some 'pseudoempirics' on this topic, see Callen et al. (1976).

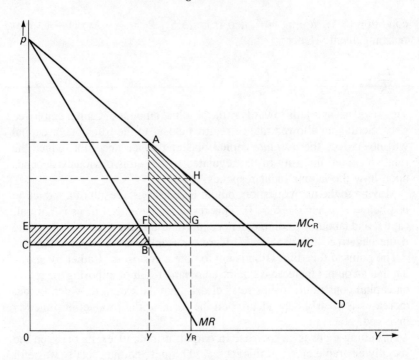

Figure 5.1   Averch–Johnson tradeoffs

Essentially, this gives rise to two possibilities. First, if the firm is able to effect an improvement in efficiency between rate revisions, then it need not reduce its prices to match. Hence profits can rise temporarily above the ceiling suggested by the capital stock, though in the longer term, efficiency improvements are likely to be consolidated into rate revisions so the benefits may be clawed back for consumers. Thus there may be a long-term incentive to overcapitalize in order to resist rate reductions. However, in the interim, since the firm benefits (or, at least, its shareholders do), there may be an incentive to engage in research to reduce costs.

The second point is that capital cannot be added into the rate base between regulatory reviews. Therefore in investing in a capital asset, though there are benefits to be gained in the future from its use (which include effects it has on the profit which may be earned), there is also the immediate cost of the firm's being unable to adjust prices to recoup investment costs. This arguably reduces the tendency, noted in the A–J model, to overinvest in capital when compared with an unconstrained firm, particularly in inflationary periods when there is pressure on rates.

In summary, although regulatory lag can have adverse effects in times of high inflation (see Kafoglis, 1983), there are potential efficiency benefits of introducing a lag into the rate-setting process. These points are discussed in Baumol and Klevorick (1970).

One other issue which has had considerable attention paid it in the literature is the influence of uncertainty upon the A—J result. Briefly, whether the A—J result is modified or not depends upon the way in which uncertainty is introduced. The regulated firm must plan to maximize expected (utility of) profit, given, say, that demand has a random element. This will involve choosing certain factors *ex ante* and allowing others to adjust given the outcome. It might seem natural to choose capital stock and let labour adjust (as in Peles and Stein's 1976 paper). However, although conventional, the reasonableness of this assumption really depends upon the industry under consideration. If the labour is skilled and conventionally has tenure, barring misdemeanour, the stock of labour cannot easily be adjusted. In that case, a more appropriate assumption may be that both labour and capital are chosen *ex ante*, hence determining output, and that price adjusts to clear the market. Alternatively, capital, labour and price may be set *ex ante* and there is either excess supply or excess demand depending upon the stochastic outcome. In both the latter two models, Das (1980) shows that the A—J result, in the form described earlier, holds good.

Finally, we should note that tests of the A—J effect have been attempted, but it is actually rather more difficult to test than appears at first sight — see Johnson (1973), also Baron and Taggart (1977).

Price regulation models

There is no model of price regulation with as established a reputation as the A—J model. We will consider here three stylized possibilities relating to actual situations. All deal in different ways with the point that price must be set by reference to something.

Most closely related to the A—J model is one in which the profit revenue ratio is regulated. In that case, we would have:

$$\text{Max } \Pi = p \cdot y(x_1, x_2) - wx_1 - rx_2 \qquad (5.7)$$

subject to

$$(py - wx_1 - rx_2)/py \leq S. \qquad (5.8)$$

Again, let us assume that the constraint is binding, whence it becomes:

$$py(1 - S) - wx_1 - rx_2 = 0.$$

Setting up the Lagrangean and differentiating, then dividing one first order
condition by the other, along the lines of equations (5.3) and (5.5), easily
yields:

$$\frac{R_2}{R_1} = \frac{w}{r}.$$

Hence then, unlike the A—J case, there is no over- (or under-)capitaliza-
tion, so no direct welfare loss for this reason. With S providing a binding
constraint reducing prices below what they would otherwise have been,
regulation of this type improves welfare by reducing the monopoly welfare
loss, at least within the context of the model. Unfortunately, there is a,
practical problem: whereas it is fairly easy for regulators to get a reasonable
idea of what constitutes a 'fair' return on capital, ideas concerning a fair
return on revenue would be rather more vague.

Assume now that regulation takes the form of allowing prices to rise
in line with costs. We will have to be specific about what we mean, because
factor prices are unlikely to rise completely in line with each other. Thus,
suppose that each factor has a weight attached to it, given by last year's
expenditure proportion. Then the ratio p_{i2}/p_{i1} (1 referring to last year, 2
to this) is applied to each input i's expenditure proportion in order to get
the new cost allowance. Prices are allowed to go up to the same proportionate extent that costs have risen.

What I have been describing is a Laspeyres (base-weighted) cost index
system. Consequently, this gives rise to the problem (well known in index
number theory; see for example, Deaton and Muellbauer, 1980, ch. 7),
that the firm finds itself continually better off until the index is revised.
The argument may be adapted from the standard one on Laspeyres price
indexes, and is illustrated by figure 5.2. The firm is currently producing
on isoquant $\bar{y}$ with isoquant line (given by prevailing factor prices) AB.
Therefore inputs 1 and 2 are used in amounts x_{11}, x_{21} respectively. Then
in period 2, factor x_1 becomes relatively expensive, factor x_2 relatively
cheap (though both may, for example, increase in price). The cost formula gives the firm enough money to buy the old factor combination at
the new relative prices, in effect allowing the firm isocost line CD. This,
however, leaves the firm better off. It could, for example, produce output
y', or it could continue to produce $\bar{y}$, but using an alternative factor combination resulting in isocost curve EF, and make more profit. Of course
in the short term there will be only limited scope for the firm to substitute
among factors, but the fact remains that this procedure leads to the regulated
firm becoming no worse, and probably better off, over time, at consumers'
expense.

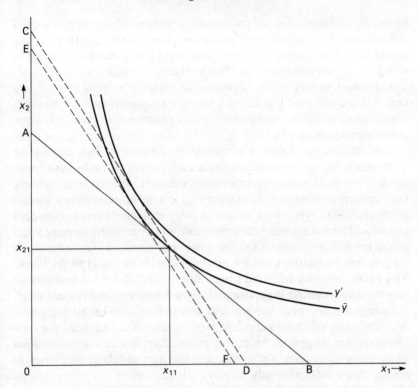

Figure 5.2 Factor price compensation effects

The final possibility, which is discussed at greater length below, is regulation in which prices are set exogenously. For example, prices may be allowed to rise by no more than the retail price index, or that minus something ('RPI − X'). Why impose some seemingly unnecessary uncertainty on the firm regarding its prices when compared with its costs? One reason, given what has gone immediately before, is to avoid guaranteeing the firm full compensation for its chosen factor combination, no matter how much some of the input prices rise with respect to others.

There is, however, another rather more important and more general reason for avoiding full compensation, as we shall see.

Underlying assumptions

The essential problem in any regulatory scheme is that the regulator knows less than the firm about the parameters facing that firm. This is why indirect forms of regulation (e.g. of profitability) are applied, but there are still difficulties even in such indirect regulation. Two implicit assumptions that are often made when they are not warranted are that 'price' is a particularly transparent observation and that costs are being minimized (given the constraints which the regulators impose). The assumption about costs in turn breaks down into two: that factor prices are exogenous and that no waste of productive factors is entertained. We must examine these implicit assumptions in more detail.

Superficially, the notion of a price gives no trouble. But suppose we were regulating the price of telephone calls. It would not be sensible to set a price of Z pence per minute, since they are not a completely homogeneous commodity. Thus if the task is to set up a regulatory scheme of the 'RPI − X' type, there would be more than one way to do it: each price could be constrained (a tiresome task, the more so the more varieties of the product in question) or, more popular, a representative basket of outputs could be defined and the price for that basket could be regulated. This causes obvious difficulties regarding goods outside the basket (e.g. new products), changes in the composition of consumers' baskets, and so on.

Though this is explicitly a problem only in the case of direct regulation of price, it rears its head indirectly in other cases. For example, in a cost-compensation framework for setting prices, there is a difficulty over joint costs common to several products, and the firm may have incentives to change the bundle of goods it offers. Under rate of return regulation, effectively the firm is free to define its basket of inputs and outputs as it sees fit, but there may be social criteria which conflict with the firm's judgement regarding the way its price schedules comply with the regulatory formula — for example it might be engaging in predatory pricing in areas vulnerable to competition.

Related to the question of price is that of quality. In many cases, a price set on (say) a per unit basis will still allow discretion to the firm in terms of how much quality is embedded in that unit. It makes no sense to regulate price closely if the firm has absolute discretion regarding quality, both because the socially desirable quality is unlikely to be the one the firm wishes to produce, and because tight regulation of price may encourage the firm to derogate quality to increase profit. Examples here might be water supply and, particularly, sewage disposal. Quality cannot be considered exogenous.

Are costs exogenous? In our models so far we have taken factor prices as given. But suppose those supplying the factors know that compensation for input price rises will be allowed, and suppose further that there are barriers to entry into factor supply, so that prices there do not align automatically with factor costs. Examples might be airline pilots and electrical generating equipment manufacturers. Here the factor prices are not exogenous, but are at least partly under the control of those supplying the factors. A situation of bilateral monopoly power could develop, where factor prices are raised above alternative use values, thereby raising marginal and average costs above what they would otherwise be. Then, through the cost compensation mechanism, final good prices could and would be increased.

This is explicitly a problem for schemes in which cost compensation at 100 per cent is built in. However, it is no less a problem in profit revenue ratio or profit return on capital schemes, assuming always that the regulated firm has scope for price rises without losing profit (i.e. price is still below the profit maximizing value). In both cases, an increase in an allowable cost is sufficient for the firm to be able to increase its prices. The only case which escapes this problem entirely is the 'RPI − X' type, since here the 'cost' trigger is exogenous.

More radically, why should the firm be assumed to be an efficient profit maximizer (and cost minimizer)? It may be that the managers of the firm do not have profit maximization as an objective. As we have seen in chapter 3, management is constrained in its actions by shareholders and other capital market constraints and in addition, perhaps, by the managerial labour market, but these constraints may be attenuated within the regulatory framework. More specifically, different forms of regulation will allow relaxation of capital market constraints to differing extents. In the discussion on this point below, I shall make use of the distinction between productive and allocative efficiency, the former relating to the efficiency of transforming input into output, the latter to the efficiency in pricing that output. Regulatory schemes have an impact on both.

Rate of return regulation (in the form represented in the A−J model) has a detrimental impact on productive efficiency in terms of creating the 'overcapitalization' bias. Arguably it also has if anything a detrimental indirect impact through dulling the incentives to efficiency arising in the capital market, so allowing costs to be higher than they might be. Supposing that the rate of return allowed is one which the firm can easily achieve, bankruptcy is unlikely to be a problem. Moreover, both shareholders and takeover raiders have little power, the former because earnings per share are at the maximum allowed level, the latter because there is no very convincing way of suggesting that the raider will improve performance in a way relevant to the shareholders.

In the profit revenue ratio regulation and cost compensation cases, it is not so clearly the case that capital market constraints are dulled since shareholders and takeover raiders are interested directly in returns on capital. However, it seems plausible that the effect of these restraints will be to give shareholders and takeover raiders limited scope for manoeuvre, and we have already noted that the incentives to efficiency are weak in the cost compensation case.

By contrast, price regulation of the 'RPI − X' type focuses less directly on allocative efficiency but may imply more effective constraints on productive efficiency. We make the former assertion since if technical economies of scale and so on were, for example, to allow prices to fall 'naturally' by some value greater than X each year, the constraint on pricing behaviour relative to costs would become weaker over time. This is possibly the case with British Telecom, who have X at 3 per cent in a technically progressive industry.

The other side of this coin is that 'RPI − X' allows companies to retain the benefits of increased efficiency as long as X remains unchanged. Conversely, assuming input prices rise roughly in line with the RPI, a refusal to change working practices will bring the firm into conflict with either the regulatory authority or its shareholders, as bankruptcy looms. Potential takeover raiders do have the opportunity to show that they could provide real benefits to shareholders whilst remaining within the regulatory constraint.

In sum, price regulation of this sort reduces greatly the 'cost plus' nature of the contract relative to all the other schemes. As a consequence, this kind of regulation should tackle the problems of cost endogeneity and incentives to efficiency more clearly than do other methods. Of course, this is at the expense of some uncertainty for the firm. If wholesale prices and market wage rates consistently outstrip the retail price index, an efficient producer would experience difficulties in meeting the formula. Assuming this problem is irrelevant, the other major question is whether the takeover mechanism is sufficiently effective and reliable to influence efficiency in a strongly positive way. Many observers (e.g. Mueller, 1980, ch. 10) consider that the benefits of takeovers are, at best, unproved, and that large firms always present difficulties for the takeover mechanism.

Finally, we may note that none of the schemes completely avoids the potential problem of 'regulatory capture' — regulators identifying with the goals of the firm. Safeguards against this relate rather more closely to the administrative mechanisms by which regulation is imposed (see section 5.3).

5.2 Extensions of the models

In the previous section, and particularly the final paragraphs, a number of questions were raised about the efficiency of particular types of regulation. In particular, I have been rather hard on the rate of return regulation and full cost compensation schemes. Nevertheless, neither profit revenue ratio control nor the 'RPI − X' schemes emerge unscathed and the latter is rather an unknown quantity, with particular problems arising if it is envisaged as operating over a considerable period of time (Littlechild, 1986, ch.10). This section will examine some issues of relevance to these latter two schemes in rather greater analytical detail.

Cost endogeneity

Here I shall take up the point made in the previous section about costs not necessarily being exogenous either to the nature of the factor inputs (through their prices) or, more specifically, to the objective of the firm and the constraints upon it. Since we have chosen to examine a case involving a symmetric constraint, there is no A−J effect and we may, for simplicity, suppress the factor proportions aspect.

Let us consider a problem of the following form, adapted from (5.7) and (5.8)

$$\left.\begin{array}{l} \text{Maximize } \Pi = p \cdot y - C(y,\omega) \\[2mm] \text{subject to} \\[2mm] \dfrac{py - C(y,\omega)}{py} \leq S \end{array}\right\} \qquad (5.9)$$

where we have suppressed factor prices in the cost function $C(\cdot)$ but included 'waste', ω. However, rather than pursuing the model (a variant of Bailey, 1973, ch. 3, and Daughety, 1984) mathematically, let us adopt a diagrammatic approach.

The workings of the model are illustrated in figure 5.3. For simplicity, we assume linear demand $D \equiv p(y) = a - by$ and constant marginal and average cost (given waste) $\partial C/\partial y = c(\omega) = c + \omega$. The constraint in (5.9) may then be written:

$$(1 - S)D = c + \omega.$$

Hence the lines $(1 - S_1)D$, $(1 - S_2)D$ represent possible constraint formulations.

Since the firm wishes to maximize profit, when no constraint is imposed marginal revenue equals marginal cost, with output and price denoted by y_u, p_u. If the relevant constraint is that associated with S_1, then with truthful cost reporting, $c(0) = c$, the minimum output and maximum price are y_1 and p_1 respectively. Now, the firm will not wish to reduce output

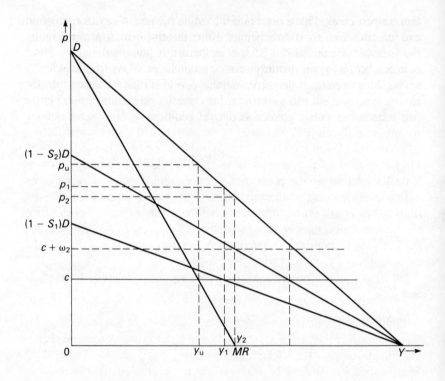

Figure 5.3   Profit maximization and waste

from this level by adjusting costs upwards since, with costs being adjustable, profit maximization is equivalent to revenue maximization. Moreover, the firm cannot increase output beyond the maximizing value y_1 to increase revenue. Therefore, (y_1, p_1) is the equilibrium outcome, and no waste is created.

Suppose now that the constraint is tightened to S_2. If the firm reported its costs truthfully, this would take it beyond the revenue maximizing point y_2. Hence there is an incentive for the firm to misreport its costs to increase revenue. By indulging in waste or 'padding' of an amount ω_2 per unit of output, output can be reduced to y_2 and price increased to p_2.[4]

One important conclusion that may be drawn from this model is that when we admit the possibility of wasteful expenditures by the firm, they are nevertheless not always present. This is a surprising conclusion, perhaps,

---

[4]This again implicitly points out the difference between the A–J overcapitalization (which is not present here) and 'gold plating' or wasteful expenditures.

but it is crucially dependent upon the implicit assumption that wasteful expenditures directly endow neither utility nor disutility to those running the firm (since only profits appear in the utility function).

In practice, however, management may gain direct utility from cost levels above the minimum if they are associated with a relatively easy life for the management. In this case firms may indulge in padding even before the maximum revenue point is reached. Additionally, and again outside the model as developed, cost padding may be created by particular factors of production bidding up their earnings above opportunity costs through the use of monopoly power exercised, for example, by a trade union or a professional association.

Practically speaking then, regulators are unlikely to know whether costs as reported are at a minimum level, unless:

(1) they take some steps to verify firm behaviour, perhaps through an independent review or using external information; or
(2) they employ some mechanism which is designed to make it in the regulated firm's best interests to reveal costs; or
(3) they can rely upon capital pressures to keep the firm's costs down.

These considerations moreover, are relevant to 'RPI − X' type schemes where periodic revisions in X are required in order to take account of changing circumstances (see Vickers and Yarrow, 1985, ch. 3). As the third qualification has already been discussed in the previous section (and in ch. 3), let us turn to the other two possibilities listed above.

Yardstick competition

An obvious source of external information is the experience of other concerns engaged in similar activities. An example would be the use of cost information generated in one water authority to regulate another authority's prices. A model based on this possibility has been developed by Shleifer (1985).

Suppose that the firm in question has a profit function of the form:

$$\Pi = (p - c)y(p) - E(c) \tag{5.10}$$

where $E(\cdot)$ is a function representing the cost of effort involved in reducing unit production costs c below some value c_0, with $E' < 0$ (lower costs involve more effort) and $E'' > 0$ (reducing costs becomes progressively more difficult). Notice that although the maximand is profits, here in effect effort involves a disutility, which makes (5.10) different from (5.9). The regulator wants to maximize social welfare, as usual the sum of consumer and producer surplus, but (in this variant) faces the problem that although the social optimum would involve pricing at marginal costs, this is infeasible since with $E(\cdot) > 0$, marginal cost pricing at c involves losses. Hence the regulator, as before, goes for average cost pricing. The other complication is that marginal costs are not fixed, which means there is another optimal condition relating to c. Since c does not appear directly in the evaluation of consumer surplus, from (5.10) we can derive the social optimality condition:

$$\frac{\partial \Pi}{\partial c} = - y(p) - E'(c) = 0 \tag{5.11}$$

(and we assume the second order conditions hold). This equates the marginal cost of a small reduction in production costs, $E' \Delta c$ to the marginal benefit, the reduction in costs $y\Delta c$. In sum, the regulator wants (5.11) to hold, along with a breakeven condition, namely:

$$(p - c)\, y(p) - E(c) = 0. \tag{5.12}$$

How is the regulator's task achieved? Suppose, for simplicity, there is another firm facing identical demand and cost conditions. The other firm has costs $\bar{c}$ and spends $\bar{E}$ on cost reduction. Thus the regulator can replace c by $\bar{c}$ and E by $\bar{E}$ in (5.12) and solve for p, which is then presented to the firm as a parameter. Accordingly, the firm minimizes costs in (5.10) by choosing c, the only variable at its disposal, obtaining condition (5.11). The values of E and c which result should exactly satisfy (5.12) since the firms are identical.

This model may seem naively simplistic, but Shleifer in fact demonstrates how it may be extended to the rather more realistic case where there is a group of firms differing in observable exogenous characteristics. Here, a regression analysis approach is used to obtain predicted cost levels for each firm separately, to apply in (5.12). He illustrates its potential applicability with reference to Medicare reimbursement expenditures in the United States. Similar types of regression schemes have been used in the UK in allocating money to the health services and also to local authorities.

Nevertheless, the model does have drawbacks. First it assumes the regulator knows the demand function facing the firm, $y(p)$. Secondly, it assumes that a regression approach is adequate to pick up all special relevant features determining costs, and all relevant features influencing cost reduction expenditures across the sample. Thirdly, the dynamics of the process are unclear. There is some implicit general notion of a period over which current costs are gathered and which then feed through to future actions. Finally, it is a crucial assumption that the regulator is the only actor indulging in strategic behaviour.

These last two points have (in effect) been taken up by Daughety (1984).

The dynamics of his process are that once the regulator has specific ground rules, the firms involved decide what prices to propose, the regulator decides whether to accept them and, assuming they are acceptable, the firms base their output decisions upon the announced price ceilings. Here there is scope for strategic coordinatory behaviour amongst the firms. Daughety analyses a case where there is a Stackleberg leader[5] in the industry and finds it suggests that such yardstick schemes still allow inefficient firms to operate and allow (in his case) the leader to misrepresent costs and so protect profits. In order for yardstick competition to work it must be very strictly the case that those forming each others' yardstick are not allowed to coordinate behaviour.

Incentive mechanisms

Rather than attempting to force the firm to reveal its true costs and their structure, the regulatory authority could try to devise a scheme in which it is in the firm's best interests to declare costs truthfully or to produce as if according to the true costs. We will consider two examples rather briefly.

Baron and Myerson (1982) consider a regulator facing a monopolist (so comparisons are impossible) whose costs he does not know. The firm is persuaded to reveal its true costs through application of a vector of policies involving price, subsidies/taxes and a probability of not being allowed to operate if its costs are 'too high'. To gain some insight into their model, we may note that one way of getting the firm to act in a socially optimal manner would be to give it (somehow) the title to all social surplus. This would be unacceptable on distributional grounds (implicitly because consumers' and producers' benefits are weighted differently). However, by making the expected demand curve faced by the firm different from the actual demand curve, that result can be replicated in effect without the firm's taking all the surplus. Suppose, for example, only marginal costs (and not fixed costs) are unknown, and suppose these vary according to a parameter θ, where $\theta_0 < \theta < \theta_1$, then the demand curve could be adjusted away from true according to the *reported* value of θ. The firm, receiving a subsidy/tax equivalent to consumer surplus under the adjusted demand curve, is induced to act in a socially optimal manner, but consumers generally benefit also since the adjusted and true demand curves differ. Some deadweight welfare loss normally arises because of the difference between the curves.

---

[5]That is, a firm which takes other firms' actions (outputs) as given and optimizes based upon these; see, for example, Waterson (1984a), for a textbook explanation.

Finsinger and Vogelsang (1981) have a version of their scheme, discussed at length in the previous chapter, which is applicable to regulated firms. In fact it could be seen as a rather unsophisticated version of the Baron and Myerson model, since it relies on the same observation that subsidizing the firm to the extent of the consumer surplus gain gives rise to an optimal result.

The essence of their scheme is that at the end of each period, t, the firm is paid a subsidy:

$$S_t = S_{t-1} + y_{t-1}(p_{t-1} - p_t). \tag{5.13}$$

This is a first order approximation to the consumer surplus gain arising in any period from the firm's decision to reduce price. Looking at figure 5.4 (which shows a case of constant marginal cost, for simplicity), we may note that the firm would be just on the margin of wanting to reduce price from monopoly, f_m, to competitive level c in one stroke, since the gain in surplus ABKJ would be precisely the loss in monopoly profit. However, reducing price first from p_m to p_2 brings with it a subsidy of ABFE in the

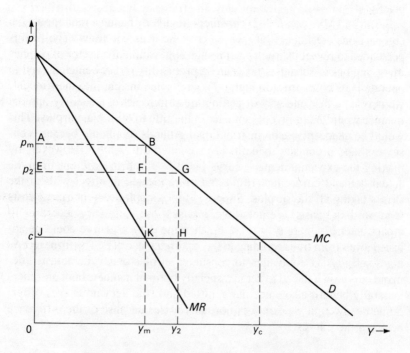

Figure 5.4 Subsidy schemes and optimality

first period, then a further reduction to c adds area EGHJ, giving a subsidy of ABFGHJ in total in the second, and subsequent, periods which is greater than the profit forgone. In fact, the more gradual the steps, the larger is the eventual subsidy, at the expense of early periods, and an infinitesimal step implies the firm captures the whole of the consumer surplus.

Note that the scheme is rather similar to the one discussed in section 4.3. The incentive to indulge in a further price reduction between periods $t-1$ and t is the algebraic sum of the difference in profits and the difference in subsidy $S_t - S_{t-1}$. Hence, from (5.13) it is:

$$I_t = \Pi_t - \Pi_{t-1} + y_{t-1}(p_{t-1} - p_t)$$

For reasons discussed in section 4.3 then, it also provides an incentive to cost reduction.

However, there is also a rather substantial point of difference regarding the distributional implications. In the public enterprise scheme, the manager benefited to the extent of a first order approximation to the *increment* in consumer surplus plus profits. Here the firm captures nearly all, and in the infinitesimal step case all, of the benefits it creates. Yet the rationale for regulation is normally not only an efficiency but also a distributional one, which goes against this scheme. In the public firm case the manager's incentive was there, albeit attenuated, even if only a fraction of I_t were paid to him directly, since he had no automatic claim to any of the surplus. Here the firm has a natural claim to the profits and if only say one-quarter of S were paid, the firm would definitely be better off earning monopoly profits and no subsidy rather than the subsidy only at a competitive price, and similarly at intermediate points. Hence this scheme suffers from the same distributional problems as did the public enterprise one, but in a more acute form.

Before concluding this section, it should be said that the models above have been developed using the assumption that the regulators are acting in the public interest. It is worth reiterating that comparison between regulatory schemes in the extent to which they allow 'capture' of the regulators by the firm is also important. This point comes more to the fore in the following section, but see also Hilton (1972) on the incentives facing regulators.

5.3 Some examples of regulatory schemes

In order to add some flesh to the bones of these theoretical models, as well as to aid appreciation of the practical problems, this section will examine some examples of regulatory schemes in industries with strong natural monopoly elements. We start with the classic rate of return type — public utility regulation in the United States — and then turn to the price control scheme in operation in the gas industry in the UK. The latter is a modified version of the 'RPI − X' scheme employed in British Telecom's regulation.

The first point to make about US utility regulation is that the Averch−Johnson framework is only a model.[6] The regulatory agency does not in fact set a maximum rate of return, though the 'rate case' is an important aspect of the state regulatory body's activities. In fact, the state Public Utility Commission (PUC) typically has wider powers, encompassing legislative activity and quasi-judicial decision-making as well as executive power (subject to appeal). Because the PUC has a dual role — public advocacy as well as decisions about rates — some states split the staff to some extent.

The rate-making process is essentially judicial in nature (see Kolbe and Read, 1984, ch. 1 for some details). Application for rate revision is made by the utility and there is a public hearing with advocates from the utility and the PUC presenting their cases. The purpose of the hearing is to determine what revenues are likely to result from the rates and to compare these with costs, sometimes on the basis of estimates for the future year, otherwise on the basis of a historic year, perhaps with adjustments for known cost increases. In making the comparison between revenues and costs, the commissioners set rates predicted to allow the utility a 'just and reasonable' return on capital assets employed. Hence the A−J model provides a simple caricature of the process.

In practice, the lesson of that model regarding padding of the rate base seems to have been well taken. One of the other main functions of the PUC is to decide whether to allow major investments (e.g. in new generating capacity) and to weigh them against alternatives such as energy conservation measures. Also, in order for investments to be allowed into the rate base they must be 'used and useful' and 'prudently' incurred. In other words, a positive decision about major investments has to be made in principle before they can be started. However, once this has happened, the investment project in question is not automatically allowed into the rate base. If it goes wrong through, for example, cost over-runs or cancellation, some PUCs will allow cost recovery over time but no return on the asset, while some others will allow no credit at all. In the latter case, the utility potentially faces bankruptcy, but in either case capital market constraints are

---

[6]The passage on the US system which follows draws fairly heavily on Brown (1986).

brought into play since the cost of bad management is borne by shareholders rather than consumers.[7]

The regulatory environment in the United States involves a considerable process of case presentation, intervention and cross-examination. This reduces the possibility of regulatory 'capture' by making for openness. Separation of the dual functions of advocacy and judicial decision-making where this has occurred and, in particular (as in California), separation of 'public interest' from 'compliance and engineering' staff, further reduce this possibility of capture. Independence from political influence is aided, in most states, by the judicial nature of appointment and by the commissioners' ability to appoint their own staff. On the other hand, this judicial process tends to be time-consuming and many states have found it necessary to lay down a maximum duration of four to six months for rate cases.

In summary, the rate regulation process, at its best, avoids many of the problems ascribed to it in the A−J model discussed earlier. Moreover it does so at reasonable (direct, at least) expense. For example, California's PUC employs around 250 people on energy utility regulation and incurs expenditure of just over 0.2 per cent of the turnover of the utilities managed. Iowa PUC has a staff of 80 and spends about 0.1 per cent of their turnover (Brown, 1986). On the other hand, rate regulation appears less able to tackle the problem of costs being comparable with those outside the regulatory sectors and has had little success in encouraging pricing policies that reduce peak demands.

Regulation of major utilities in the UK is, as yet, in its infancy. However, two principles seem to have been established, both against US tradition. First, the basis of regulation is price as compared with a general price index rather than rate of return, though with modifications particularly in the case of gas.[8] Secondly, the regulatory authority follows the Office of Fair Trading pattern (hence Oftel, Ofgas), with a Director General at its head as decision-taker, rather than adopting a quasi-judicial framework. Thus there is no separation of monitoring and advocacy from judgement nor, it appears, any judicial appeal procedure, though Littlechild (1986) claims nevertheless that the lesser degree of contact makes 'regulatory capture' less likely (a claim which appears so far to have been borne out in the case of Oftel).

---

[7]In addition to these roles, the PUC, like similar bodies in the UK, has day-to-day monitoring, safety checking, consumer complaint and auditing functions, none of which is really our concern.

[8]An exception to this is the regulation of condom prices in the UK, which was essentially on the rate of return, see Monopolies and Mergers Commission (1982).

Price regulation in the gas industry is based upon the 'RPI – X' formula, first used for telephone services, but with some additional noteworthy features. The actual formula for determining the price of gas is:

$$M_t = (1 + RPI_t^* - X)P_{t-1} + Y_t^* - K_t$$

where M_t is the maximum allowed price per therm, P_{t-1} is the amount per therm of non-gas costs (labour, capital, etc.) in the previous year, X is the fraction (currently 0.02) by which price rises must be lower than the RPI (also written as a fraction) and Y_t is the allowable gas cost per therm. In order to arrive at the value for M_t, the British Gas Corporation (BGC) is required to predict RPI and Y (hence the asterisk, for predicted values). If its predictions turn out wrong, the final term, a correction factor, K, is activated. BGC is not required to charge M_t. If the price per therm that it sets is below M_t or if it underpredicts the RPI or gas costs, it can later raise its prices through the application of a negative K_t, whereas if it overpredicts gas costs or the RPI, K becomes positive and M_t falls. There are, in addition, provisions for penalty interest to be charged for overprediction, also provisions for only limited amounts of catching up to be allowed to reduce the possibility of predatory behaviour.

The gas industry formula gives complete compensation for average (not marginal) price rises in the raw material, unlike the telephone case. It is thus a hybrid of the exogenous-based and cost-based approaches to price regulation. Other inputs are subject to efficiency constraints, but materials are not. Presumably the argument is that the company in principle has no control over raw material prices (being valued at world prices?), though this is not self-evidently the case, since the BGC has an exploration wing and sells some gas to itself.

The other notable feature is that this formula applies only to tariff sales of gas. It does not therefore take into account customers using more than 25,000 therms a year (some of whom would be medium sized firms with little countervailing bargaining power). Such features can lead to distortions in price relativities etc. (see Bailey, 1973). More importantly for domestic consumers, it fails to take account of standing charges for the supply of gas, although British Gas must attempt to keep increases in standing charges at or below increases in the RPI (Energy Committee, 1986, para. 38). In other words, the formula has the simplicity of applying to an essentially homogeneous commodity so that no 'basket' calculation is involved, but it does not cover peripheral but important aspects of customer costs, and it is not clear that safeguards regarding non-regulated charges are adequate.

In comparing such price regulation schemes with rate of return regulation in practice, it might be argued that it is the style of regulation as much as what is regulated which differs between the United States and the UK since both systems focus on price setting. Price regulation arguably requires less information and is more transparent in its application, though on the other hand there is much less formal public debate about the issues involved, and 'regulatory capture', if it arose, would be more difficult to observe. It can be argued (e.g. Littlechild, 1986) that the burden of regulation is lighter in the UK framework, and casual evidence supports this. To give an example, Oftel employs around 100 full-time staff (Carsberg, 1986) mainly to regulate BT, which had a turnover of £8387 million in the year ending March 1986, while we have already noted the Iowa PUC employs 80 people to regulate utilities with a turnover of $3000 million (Brown, 1986). Although it is undoubtedly easier to regulate one rather than many firms, two to three times as many staff per unit of turnover is substantial. In addition, it is possible that costs incurred by companies who are the subject of regulation are also higher within the US framework.

As a final point of comparison, this time with the previous chapter, note that price regulation *could* be applied to a state-owned concern as much as to a privately owned one. But, what happens if the firm breaks the rules regarding price regulation or is unable to meet its commitments as a result of price regulation? The natural occurrence in the private sector would at first sight appear to be revocation of the licence. However, it is difficult to imagine in practice that this would take effect with, say, BGC, and one could imagine negotiations taking place regarding revision of the formula, rather than bankruptcy being contemplated.

Notes on the literature

The literature in this area is again voluminous, and I will have to be selective. On the Averch−Johnson model, Zajac (1970) provides a useful geometric treatment, Baumol and Klevorick (1970) provide a summary, Johnson (1973) gives an interim assessment and Bailey (1973) develops a comprehensive set of models. There are several useful books of readings on more detailed matters, including Crew (1979), Mitchell and Kleindorfer (1980) and Danielsen and Kamerschen (1983). Less material on price regulation has developed so far. Again Bailey is useful, also, on more practical aspects, Vickers and Yarrow (1985, ch. 3) on telecommunications and Hammond et al. (1985) and Newbery (1986) on British Gas.

6

Bidding Schemes

The essential problem we have faced throughout the book is as follows: some monopoly element in production is desirable because of the nature of the industry, yet monopoly has to be controlled, and may be inefficiently operated. One way to break this circle is to act upon the distinction between competition in the market and competition for the market. Competition for the right to serve as the monopolist seems to provide the benefits of both. The purpose of this chapter is essentially to discuss this proposition.

Section 6.1 outlines the basic idea in more detail and introduces the potential problems with bidding schemes. One of these receives rather more extensive treatment in section 6.2. Section 6.3 then looks at two specific examples in order to illustrate the practical aspects of the workings of such schemes, together with their difficulties.

6.1 Bidding for the right to supply

The essence of the bidding technique is simple and is perhaps best explained through a close analogy. Suppose you wish to employ a firm to install or modify the central heating in your home, or as another example that you want to move to another house and require someone to move your furniture. These are in essence natural monopoly problems, since it is most unlikely that it would be efficient for two or more firms actually to do the jobs involved. Such problems are normally solved by making use of the distinction between competition *in* the field and competition *for* the field. You would invite two or three or four firms to submit quotations for the work. They will know they are competing with other firms, that there is competition for the field. Hence, if they want the contract they will be induced to offer a low price. You then choose the one offering the lowest price (and satisfactory service, on which see later) to be the sole supplier, knowing that they are held to their price.[1] The mechanism is widespread and well understood.

Making the analogy is in principle straightforward. Suppose now you are a city or some larger region inviting bids for water or gas supply, or a telephone service, a television service, or a bus service. You issue an offer to tender, obtain some quotations, and choose the one offering the lowest price, or rather the best value. This all seems straightforward, and yet it is rarely done explicitly; one of my main aims is to discuss why. First though, to avoid confusion, note that there is a crucial difference between the mechanism here (sometimes called a 'Chadwick auction') and the mechanism underlying, say, the government's auctioning of oil exploration rights. In that case, the blocks go to the highest bidders — the state is acting as a monopolist attempting to get high prices and is uncaring about any consequent welfare losses. By contrast, in our case the state or city authority is acting as a consumers' agent, and so wants low prices. If both are equally cost-efficient, the latter clearly dominates (see, for example, Posner, 1972, for a discussion.)

Summarizing the position slightly more formally, franchise bidding makes a market more *contestable* than it would otherwise be. As we saw in chapter 2, contestability is essentially concerned with the absence of sunk costs and the specific nature of interactions, namely that potential entrants can move into the industry and undercut the established firm, before the latter has time to react. In most franchise bidding schemes it is possible to separate out from the competition at least some of the sunk cost element, so lessening a potential entrant's need for a prior commitment, as we shall see later. Additionally, bidding schemes normally make the 'rules of the contest' between incumbent and potential suppliers fairer than in the case where no control mechanism for entry is present. That is, an efficient new entrant with a winning bid can take on the entire market immediately rather than winning it over gradually, and in a sealed-bid auction (theoretically) there is no scope for established firm reactions to entry attempts. Hence franchise bidding has potentially powerful efficiency advantages over normal entry mechanisms. In turn, this should serve to moderate the behaviour of incumbents. However, such schemes are not without difficulties.

Essentially there are at least five potential problems with franchise bidding schemes of the type under discussion, these being of varying

---

[1]Notice one essential difference between this form of contract and the purchase, say, of a packet of cornflakes or a new car, namely that the buyer specifies the product rather than choosing from a range that sellers have on offer.

significance. They are: how many bids to solicit, the efficiency of the winning bid, how to evaluate the submissions received, how to enforce the contract, and for how long to offer the contract. The last of these is furthest away from the analogy of a standard contract we started with above, and is the subject of a separate section. The other four issues are discussed immediately below.

The number of bids

When moving house or buying a central heating system, one normally uses a rule of thumb or a convention in deciding upon the number of people to approach. For example, your new employer may insist upon three written estimates being obtained in order that assistance with removal expenses be given. One may start looking for a central heating supplier with the aim of getting four quotations, but in the end, and after some difficulty, settle for two, plus a verbal estimate.

The reason for asking for more than one quotation (even if that one does not know he is alone in being approached), is fairly obvious. Auction theory strongly suggests that the expected lowest price offer falls as the number of bidders is increased. To see this, assume that bidders' prices are arranged on a spectrum from £100 to £200 (say), but that the position of any particular potential supplier is unknown. Consider drawing increasingly large samples at random from this population. As the sample is increased by one, the lowest price bid cannot increase and will usually decrease. Empirical evidence (Brannan et al., 1984), bears out the prediction that the winning bid falls as the number of bidders rises. Yet there is a force which acts in the other way, called the 'winner's curse'. Assume that no one potential supplier knows the exact profitability of the prospect but that most strongly suspect it would be unprofitable below, say, £125. As more drawings from the distribution are made, it is more likely that a firm offering below £125 is picked up, and so chosen. This firm may then subsequently find the contract is unprofitable, but is bound on price. To avoid being chosen only when the contract is unprofitable, bidders will tend to err on the side of caution. This partially counteracts the first force. Thus although the *average* bid is likely to rise as the number of bidders increases, assuming they know the (likely) extent of competition, the expected *winning* bid falls.

This analysis suggests that you should get as many quotations as possible for a job in order to get the best price. However, things are not that straightforward, for two reasons. First, even assuming quotations are 'free' to the customers, there are costs in obtaining them: arranging appointments, discussing requirements and evaluating the tenders. This is true whether we are considering the domestic examples or a state/local authority franchise. But of course producing tenders does cost money. Supposing that each firm considering bidding knows how many other firms are in the competition, then it can evaluate its expected return and set the tender price accordingly. (For example, with a one in six chance of winning the contract, the firm has a five in six chance of making a loss equal to the bid preparation costs, so in order for entry to be worthwhile, the expected value of a win must exceed this.) Having more firms in the competition can increase rather than reduce the expected winning bid if firms' costs of supply are all very close, so that bids are clustered, and in additon if extensive bid preparation costs are built into the bids. In other words, if bidders are able to internalize the joint externality they face in providing 'free' bids, the earlier result does not necessarily hold and the lowest expected bid may be obtained when only a relatively small number of bids are invited (Samuelson, 1985; see also French and McCormick, 1984). Internalization is likely when firms know the identities of their rivals and are repeatedly coming up against them. The point here is very much akin to Posner's (1975) argument concerning expenditures directed towards capturing monopoly rents. This line of reasoning may underlie those methods of awarding contracts where in order to reduce contract prices there is a prebid round after which contractors are invited on to selected lists of those asked to tender.

Of course, all this is predicated on the assumption that bidders (though recognizing their interdependence) are genuinely independent, but they may in some cases act collusively in producing tenders, perhaps arranging amongst themselves who is to win any particular contract. This is not a superficial criticism — the 'great electrical conspiracy' in the United States (see, for example, Clarkson and Miller, 1982, pp. 332–3), which involved collusive bids to supply to public utilities, and cable-makers in the UK who supplied collusive tenders to the Post Office (see Director General of Fair Trading, 1980, p. 89) are examples. Any bid evaluation procedure will have to attempt to guard against such actions.

Efficiency of the winning bid

Demsetz' rediscovery (1968) of the 'Chadwick auction' process described above is of considerable importance. However, criticism quickly came from Telser (1969 and subsequent papers) on the grounds that, at best, the method results in getting an average-cost price quotation. Average-cost prices are not ideal. If there are no distortions elsewhere in the economy, or if this sector is sufficiently separate, marginal costs should be the aim, as we have already noted in a number of places. The Demsetz reply to this criticism is that if the difference between marginal and average cost is substantial, bidders should be required to offer multipart tariffs along the lines, say, of those in chapter 4. Then the question comes, who should evaluate the tariffs? For Posner (1972), this is solved by having bidders sign contingent contracts with potential customers. An alternative is for the government to choose.

Once multipart tariffs are envisaged, there is a general problem about how the various packages should be evaluated. Suppose the choice between alternative packages is to be made on the basis of a simple majority vote, or to be made by a vote-maximizing government. For example, consider two packages each distinguishing between two consumer groups. The first package involves a charge of £1 for class A customers, £20 for class B customers, the second a charge of £1.10 for class A, £2 for class B. Then if there are more class A than class B customers, the former package will be chosen. Naturally, firms will seek to offer attractive packages, but it is not clear that the vote-maximizing package is the socially efficient one, since intra-marginal effects cannot be taken into account completely. Thus even with all other things in its favour, the pricing scheme chosen will be unlikely to be fully efficient in cases, such as are our concern, where scale economies are important.

Evaluating the contract

We have just discussed the problem of pricing where average cost is un-equal to marginal cost, and by extension the problem of evaluating a con-tract in which there is more than one 'price'. There is naturally a diffi-culty also where a whole range of products is to be supplied, the more so when products differ across bidders. But quality problems are also central to the question of evaluation; for example, will the cheap removal firm be insured, should it break something you cherish?

The task of the agency evaluating a franchise contract is to choose the one that provides the best deal. But what does this mean? Almost inevitably (again) value judgements come into play in making the selection. Besides the problem of weighting different classes of customer, there are issues such as: would consumers of a television service want longer programm-ing hours or higher quality programmes; should imported shows be restricted to a certain percentage of total output; how much local content should there be? Or, in the case of a bus service, should the cheaper but less frequent offer be preferred to the more expensive but more frequent service, and what about comfort and safety? To be sure, some of these judgements can be resolved by reference to established research (e.g. on the value of a 'time−cost tradeoff' — see, for example, Beesley, 1965 — for bus fre-quency against price), but others cannot.

In general, there is the question of how closely the evaluator/regulator should specify what is required (that is, make the judgements *ex ante*) and how much specification should be left to the professional judgement of the bidders, each attempting to produce what they see as an unbeatable package. There are many examples where the specification of the award-ing body incorporate a wide range of things which are bound to raise the supply price, but which are not clearly essential. Examples range from cable television systems to (in a different sphere) weapons systems.

Related to this question is the hidden assumption that both the evaluator and the bidder know the technology and the market involved. For example, in the case of cable TV, does the evaluator know about the general rela-tionship between cost structure and the number of channels to be provided, or does the potential supplier know enough about the neighbourhoods in-volved to be able accurately to predict take-up? The early history of com-mercial television in the UK demonstrates that the ITA (now IBA), who issued contracts, underestimated its profitability, whilst more recently, the IBA overestimated the profitability of commercial radio. Unforeseen aspects of technology also may create problems, as is perhaps more commonly seen in the cases of weapons systems and civil engineering works than in the sort of franchise contracts we are considering.

Enforcement

This leads to the question of enforcing the contract. Again, we will examine this first using the analogies previously developed. In the case of the domestic central heating example, if the contractor's performance is un-satisfactory, there are fairly clearly established procedures for obtaining a remedy. Assuming it is clear that the customer was not withholding something about what was required and is keeping to his or her side of the bargain (e.g. in allowing the contractor unrestricted access to the premises), he or she should be able successfully to prosecute a civil action resulting in the award of sufficient damages to enable the initially con-tracted specification to be fulfilled at the quoted price.

Things are more difficult in the case of a weapons system or civil engineer-ing contractor. Suppose the weapons system contractor runs into problems with the software, or suppose that a hit on the target can only be guaranteed if the target happens to be of the type current when the system was designed but now superseded and obsolete. Again, suppose the civil engineering contractor hits unexpectedly unfavourable terrain, or suppose traffic forecasts now suggest that a modified design should be built. There are two points to these examples. First, it is not always clear who is to blame for the problem. Secondly, if execution of the contract in accord with the

original quotation has proved extremely unprofitable in the light of experience, it is most unlikely that an alternative contractor would be willing
to step in.

If the contract proves problematic in one of the above ways what is the
government (or whoever offered it) to do? One 'solution' would be to pay
the original contractor as little as possible for work done to date, and to
re-let the contract. But the original contractor at least has the benefit of
experience, so that it might be cheaper to renegotiate the contract with
the original contractor than remove them summarily. In addition, employing
a new contractor is likely to lead to further delays in completion. Hence,
at any given stage it might seem that the expected future costs of continuing with the incumbent contractor outweigh the benefits, yet nevertheless
there may be considerable cost and time over-runs.

So, if the contract is surrounded by manifold uncertainties, there is a
fair likelihood that the original specification will not be met in one or another
dimension. But then, if potential contractors know this is likely, and know
that the issuer of the contract knows this is likely, the bids received will
tend to be very optimistic regarding price, completion date, and so on,
since the bidders expect that they can obtain extra payments in the course
of the contract. The whole situation becomes like a game of sequential
decision-making between principal and agent (and has been modelled as
such by Lewis, 1986). In summary, the initial specifications must be
recognized as being somewhat optimistic, and must be evaluated in that
light, in cases where uncertainties are important in magnitude.

The situation in franchise bidding of the type we are considering involves
a similar confounding of risks and decisions. The suppliers of a TV service or a cable network may have to compromise on quality or raise price
compared with their original specification. Again, then, the question of
termination is important. The evaluator's task does not stop once the contract has been let, but must continue through overseeing the project and,
if necessary, deciding that performance is so much below what was expected
that termination will be necessary. Such a decision is made particularly
burdensome in the case of utility supply (e.g. water or gas) since emergency
arrangements will be required to ensure continuing supply.

This question of when performance must be terminated leads us to the
topic of the next section, namely the length and type of contract that should
be awarded.

6.2 Contract type and contract length

Essentially, there are two types of contract which can be offered, namely
a complete franchise (inclusive of investment decisions) or an operating

franchise. For example, suppose there are plans for a service station on a new motorway. Bids could either be invited for the construction and operation of this station for a period of years, or the motorway authorities could build the facility and then invite bids for the operating franchise. In the former case, there is the obvious question of what happens to the asset at the time when the first franchise draws to an end. This question will occupy us for much of this section. For the moment though, we will stay with the operating franchise.

Operating franchises

Analytically, an operating franchise has a rather novel structure. In terms of the principal–agent framework of chapter 3, if we view the 'public' as the principal, then the relevant government body is the agent as far as investment decisions are concerned, but the franchisee is the agent in relation to operating decisions. Therefore there is room for potential conflict between the government in its role of acting for the public and its role as investor in capital facilities (with the latter arm perhaps eager to improve facilities for long-term gain but the former taking the view that funds are presently overstretched). There is also scope for conflict between the state-owned investment arm and the privately owned operating facility, just as there are disputes between landlords and tenants. For example, the operator has no particular incentive to treat the facilities carefully and has an incentive to push the view that the facilities are inadequate and should be improved, whereas the government may be reluctant to improve them without a performance guarantee. Yet the efficient performance of the enterprise as a whole depends upon coordination between the asset and the operating managements.

One of the major problems to be resolved in this type of arrangement is the formula for risk-sharing. The demand for the facility and the costs of supplying it will necessarily be subject to some uncertainty. Moreover it is unlikely that the ultimate authority will be able to observe (or interpret) the detail of the actions taken by asset and operating managements. Therefore, even with risk-averse operators, some risk-sharing is required in order to reduce moral hazard problems, as we saw in chapter 3 (and see also Shavell, 1979). But what of the nature of risk-sharing between asset and operating managements? It is clear that neither a constant rental paid for use of the asset, nor a pure royalty based upon final revenues, or units of output, will suffice to ensure coordination. The constant rental bears too heavily on the operator when demand falls below expectations, whilst the royalty provides little incentive to boost demand and supply facilities efficiently.

Nevertheless, these problems are not unique to franchise situations. There are obvious substantial risk-sharing problems in the face of uncertain demand between an aero engine manufacturer deciding how much development effort to put into engines for a new aeroplane, and the airframe assembler. The major novelties in operating franchises are perhaps that the asset is in effect owned by the body awarding the franchise and that the 'game' is not necessarily played on a number of occasions between the same players.

The major conceptual advantage of the operating franchise framework is that it places the operation in an almost perfectly contestable setting. Not only do regular sealed bids ensure that the market can be taken over, the virtual absence of sunk costs puts a potential entrant in an almost identical position to the incumbent, so the more efficient should emerge as the victor. I say virtual absence because, although the operator by definition needs no capital other than that which is relatively mobile or for which a non-negligible secondhand market exists, nevertheless there may be differences. Most obviously, in operating the franchise, the management and employees will have gained some idiosyncratic knowledge which may place the incumbent in a better position than the potential entrant. However, the potential entrant may envisage employing most of those currently employed by the incumbent, in which case such knowledge is probably transferred also. (The question then comes: how different is the new contractor?) Rather than discussing these points further in abstract terms, I shall return to them in the next section in connection with specific examples.

Complete contracts: the contract length question

As soon as discussion turns to complete contracts, asset valuation problems begin to intrude. Compounded with these are the inherent uncertainties about the future. There are essentially two compromise solutions to these problems, incomplete long-term contracts and recurrent short-term contracts, associated with the names of Demsetz and Posner respectively.

Recurrent short-term contracts to a large degree circumvent the problem of uncertainty. If you are contracting to supply electricity or a cable TV service for the next one or two years, it is fair to expect you to specify your tariffs exactly, or at least to describe fully the limited range of circumstances under which your tariffs will be modified, and the formula involved in any such modification. After all, this is essentially what holiday tour operators in the UK do when they issue brochures in September for holidays the following summer.

Where such contracts fall down is over the asset valuation problem. If you expect to control the assets only for a year or two, and if they are in workable condition, there is little incentive to invest in improving them.

Eventually though, the problem of asset removal will arise, and with it the question of what happens if your contract is not renewed. The successful bidder has two choices: to buy the assets from you or to construct new assets. But since your assets are a largely sunk cost, if you refuse to sell them, the potential entrant who will have to build his own is in an unfavourable position compared to you in bidding for the contract; your marginal cost of supply is lower than his. Perhaps, then, the nature of the scheme might include a provision forcing the sale of fixed assets to the successful bidder (and their purchase by that bidder). But at what price? Valuation problems in such cases are likely to be severe. Consider for example the franchise for an electricity distribution system, where its owner will want to be paid an amount equal to the cost of building an equivalent system, whereas the purchaser will want to pay a price as close to the scrap value as possible.

Incomplete long-term contracts ameliorate some of the problems. Over a longer period, say ten years, most substantial investments are likely to be worthwhile. To put it another way, the incumbent may have plant in place at the moment, but he would have to consider replacing this at some point in the new contract period, were he awarded the contract. Thus both incumbent and entrant will have to make substantial investments, albeit perhaps at different points in time, so that *ex ante* competition extends to a wider spectrum of activities than in the case of short-run contracts. Nevertheless, valuation problems in the case of very long-lived assets are likely to remain, and there is the question of human capital embodied in employees.

Problems arising as a result of uncertainty substantially increase over those encountered with short-term contracts when we consider incomplete long-term contracts. Williamson (1976) points to two major areas where these problems emerge. First there is the criterion for awarding the contract. It is not possible with a long-term contract for price to be specified in a simple way. For example, factor prices will vary substantially in both absolute and relative terms over the period, making the use even of a formula (like $RPI - X$) difficult. Demand is also subject to some uncertainty, so that any price schedule might have to be conditional upon demand forecasts, given the scale economies involved. Vague promises regarding price may be the most that bidders would offer. Quality also is a problem since the franchisee will make investment decisions that are likely to impact upon quality, notably relative to interruptions in service. Again, at the outset only vague promises can be made. But then there is the general question over how to evaluate the bids, for example in choosing between a bid that is rather specific in its promises of cheap supply but says little about quality, and a bid that is long on quality promises and short regarding pricing policy. The value judgements of the awarding body are bound to come into play.

As Williamson says, there is then an artificial or obscure initial award criterion.

The second major problem is concerned with enforcement and execution. In the case of a very short contract, little is gained by the firm which steps seriously out of line, because it knows the contract will then not be renewed and, if necessary, the assets can be seized by the regulatory authority prior to the formal contract termination date. The essential difficulty with the long-term contract is that this sanction of seizure is too strong for most minor breaches of the agreement, yet there is no obvious lesser sanction. No firm will install long-lived assets if they are sequestered at the slightest provocation, yet fining a company which steps out of line would seem somewhat arbitrary and likely to lead to litigation. Moreover, Williamson points out, officials who chose the company in the first place are unlikely to want to admit freely that they made a mistake. Hence persuasion is likely to be the main method of action against the franchisee in the early stages of the contract.

Because the contract is unspecific, as we said earlier, price and quality promises will not automatically be kept (does the difficulty lie with the lack of demand or in a lack of efficiency?) and it will be difficult for the awarding and overseeing body to decide when to start 'acting tough'. Moreover, this difficulty does not disappear when the overseers come to evaluating a new round of applications. Experience with the incumbent may have been bad, but the other applicants may largely be untried and so unknown quantities, and they may in practice turn out worse.

A summary example

The essence of franchising as an approach to the natural monopoly problem is that in principle it removes or minimizes the element of bilateral bargaining between buyers' agent and seller, in which the former is thought commonly to get the worst of the deal. However, if sunk costs are important and if bidders are few, there may still be substantial scope for bargaining of the type we have described above. The example developed below illustrates this in a simple algebraic manner.

Suppose that in order to carry out the contract if it is awarded, a contractor anticipates making expenditures on fixed equipment equal to an amount F on an annualized basis. (We might think of F as the payments to the finance company.) Performing the contract will in addition involve incurring variable costs C per annum. The lowest bid that can be expected for the contract thus is $B_1 = F + C$. If the investment in fixed equipment is made but is then not used for the purposes of fulfilling this contract, it can be scrapped, with the salvage value being S when written in annualized form, or it may have some alternative use in which it is valued at A_2. Obviously, $S \leq A_2 \leq F$. The next lowest bid B_2, is an amount D_1 ($= B_1 - B_2 > 0$) above B_1, so the contract is awarded to firm 1 at B_1 (if such a firm exists).

Let us suppose now that the winning firm gets into difficulties (or claims that it has got into difficulties) at the original price, and wants to raise its pricing scale. Clearly, it can go up to B_2 without much difficulty, because it is still providing the best bargain. However, under some circumstances, it can go up as far as $B_2 + (F - A_2)$, depending upon the original contract. If the government is worried about performance of the contractor, it may want to take the contract away and give it to another firm, presumably firm 2. But then the contractor can ask for (and may, dependent upon the contract wording, demand) compensation. The maximum value this can take is $F - A_2$ ($\leq F - S$), the difference between construction cost and alternative use. Hence if the government is faced with a demand for a price rise to somewhere near $B_2 + (F - A_2)$, it may still concede if it believes full performance will be forthcoming at that price, and is not confident that it would win a compensation case, particularly since the firm 2 is to some extent an unknown quantity.

The upshot is that the maximum difference between what the government ideally wants price to be and what the firm might hope to get away with eventually is $D_1 + (F - S)$. In the ideal world of franchises, this magnitude is small. $F - S$, or rather $F - A_2$, is not significant because the facilities they will employ are not unique to this contract but rather can be applied elsewhere without difficulty, so sunk costs are negligible. D_1 is similarly small because competitive bidding is in operation and competition is keen. However, not all worlds are ideal. In practice there may be few competitors and they may have to invest heavily in unique facilities.

The argument can be adapted to illustrate valuation problems arising from one firm's takeover of the contract from another. The new firm will want to pay as near to S as possible. The outgoing incumbent will want to represent, first that A_2 is substantially larger than S and secondly that F is the amount to be paid. Indeed if, for some reason, the value of the new contract is increased over the old, or the current annualized cost of investment is above F, then the incumbent may argue for more than F. Therefore the bargainers may in practice start some way from each other in their views on the value of the fixed assets.

Taken together with some additional common sense points, this example suggests some general lessons regarding franchising. If demand is fairly well known and not subject to major fluctuations, if the technology is well established and understood by bidders, if the cost structure is known and not likely to be subject to major fluctuations, then there are likely to be several serious bidders. If they have or can easily obtain (and if necessary, resell) any specialized equipment, the prospects look good on the supply side. If the technology and cost structure are well understood also by the evaluating authority, if there is an absolute standard for quality or if it is easily specified (because it has few dimensions) then the demand side also looks favourable. Thus franchising is neither useless nor, as it appears at first blush, a uniquely important solution to the natural monopoly problem.

Having said all that, early experience with contracting out of cleaning and laundering facilities in state-owned institutions such as hospitals in the UK has been mixed at best, with some contracts being rescinded at short notice (TUC, 1984), despite these operations being seemingly straightforward. This may be a learning problem or it might indicate further difficulties we have not considered.

In order to gain a greater insight into the practical aspects, we will consider two examples in more detail in the next section (but see also section 7.2 on empirical studies).

6.3 Two practical examples

The two examples I have chosen to illustrate the workings of franchising possibly do not appear the most central, but they do both have the substantial merit of having had an extensive run, including more than one contract 'round', so that teething problems have largely been ironed out. Neither has worked to everyone's satisfaction, so that both illustrate some of the problems of franchising schemes. They are US cable TV (CATV) and UK independent television franchises, respectively.

Williamson (1976) presents a detailed and rather sorry tale of a particular cable TV franchise arrangement in which, at least in the initial round, almost everything that could have gone wrong did so. The original specification and the invitation to bid were quite carefully drafted, with the bid for a basic service being limited to specifying a price, automatic fines for late completion, a surety bond, and outline specification of the technical capabilities being featured. The bids received covered an unexpectedly broad range of prices, from which the lowest was chosen, but that firm soon amalgamated with another. Demand proved substantially different from expected; specifically, takeup was low, but within that demand for more than the basic system (initially specified in vague terms only) was high. Construction was slow and the original contract was very substantially renegotiated, with each of the main dimensions moving extensively in the company's favour — capacity was reduced, non-compliance fines were reduced and charges were increased in several cases. Quality problems with the system also arose. Though termination was at one stage considered, it was rejected by the awarding office. In other words, considerable compromises away from the original franchise were introduced.

Of course this is only a single case, and franchising remains the principal mechanism for cable TV provision, but other writers have pointed to more general problems that come up in franchising in this industry. Posner (1972) notes that potentially there are three levels of government involved: municipalities, the state, and the federal authorities, and further that their objectives differ substantially. Stelzer (1983) points to three general difficulties which have arisen at later stages of the cable franchising process.

First, Stelzer notes that where contracts are awarded for extensive periods (15–20 years), as is common in this sphere, substantial expenditures have been incurred by contestants competing for the (presumably lucrative) contracts. He quotes the case of Denver, where $3 million was spent by the contestants. Obviously, as has been pointed out already, bidding costs are nontrivial, but this level of expenditure suggests competition for some monopoly element in the rent, along Posnerian (1975) lines.

Secondly, and perhaps because of the perceived profitability of cable TV, local authorities awarding franchises have demanded, or have been offered, extensive free services to local community groups and activities, huge channel capacities, payments to the municipality and so on. The provision of such facilities is argued to have increased considerably the charges to subscribers, Stelzer suggests by an average 22 per cent. Posner (1972) believes this aspect of a municipality's behaviour is endemic to the system; the municipal authority wants to see a clear return to itself from cable.

Thirdly, long period franchises are problematic in the face of rapid technical change and increasing demand for channels. Whereas the first systems supplied relatively few channels, technical improvements now mean that systems supplying very much larger numbers of channels cost very little extra to install. Hence, awarding an exclusive franchise to one firm early on subsequently causes problems for the awarding body and to customers, since there may be eager suppliers of larger capacity systems for which there is now a demand. The natural monopoly properties of the system can change over time.

Commercial TV franchises in the UK have been awarded in three rounds including that in which such broadcasting first began in 1955. The franchises are essentially regionally based (more so after the first round) and the structure is such that some areas are bound to be more profitable than others. This is reflected in the competition, where some franchises have involved several competitors — five in some instances — whilst others have remained with an unopposed incumbent. The structure of the franchises on offer has changed to some extent over time, with marginal changes between areas (and, in the London area, times), the introduction of a separate

breakfast TV service etc. Also there have been several changes in the identities of the successful applicants; for example, the 1980 round saw the
removal of two incumbents and their replacement by outsiders, plus the
reconstitution of one major operator (Central) and the separation of ownership structure between two others (Yorkshire and Tyne–Tees).

One interesting feature of the structure is that the companies do not own
the transmitters they use but rather pay rentals for the right to use them.
This undoubtedly reduces the sunk cost element and so makes it easier
for an outsider to enter the contest. However, it arguably leads to relative
inefficiencies in the provision of transmission services (Domberger and
Middleton, 1985).

Another feature that provides a natural contrast with the US cable system
is that there is no 'price' element as such in the bidding. Hence companies
compete on the basis of promises regarding quality, usually backed up with
lists of prominent personalities who will be associated with the station.
This makes for difficulty in judging between contestants, and indeed the
criteria for franchise awards are not specified in any very explicit way.
Lewis (1975) makes several substantive criticisms of the 1967 round of
awards, including the point that unsuccessful incumbents had little warning or expectation that their reappointments would not be a formality. To
many eyes the ousted incumbents did not appear clearly worse than those
who won. He also (implicitly) endorses Williamson's theoretical point that
putative franchisees have little guidance as to what is being sought (1976).

There is the additional question (which arose in discussing cable above)
of what is to happen if the promises turn out to be false or if they cannot
be maintained in the face of low revealed demand. The new breakfast TV
service TV–AM ran into difficulties in early 1983 and drastic economies
were made, personalities dropped and new management introduced. The
IBA (the awarding body) did not step in to revoke the licence, though it
may have negotiated on compromises. Previously, a new contractor, London
Weekend, ran into difficulties shortly after being awarded a franchise, but
was not removed. The IBA has acted, however, so as to prevent mergers
between the companies it has licensed and what it sees as undesirable suitors.

In general, Lewis (1975) considers that it is the nature of the institutional structure that has been created and evolved, rather than the concept
of franchising itself, which gives rise to the criticisms he has of IBA programme contract awards. Indeed, he sees the IBA learning from some of
its mistakes in its approach to local radio.

Turning to inter-company relations, it is interesting to observe their
negotiations regarding the main fixed capital assets, that is their studios
and the human resources employed therein, which occur when franchises
change hands. Domberger and Middleton (1985) detail the bargaining

postures adopted by the two 1980 incumbents and their successors, in which the incumbents attempt to demonstrate that studios have alternative uses, whilst the entrants set in motion their acquisition of new facilities. In the event, the new firm bought the old one's studios in both cases, and many staff simply transferred their employment to the new company. Williamson's asset transfer problems arise, but in these cases it seems they are not insoluble.

Unfortunately, the contract length question has not been resolved satisfactorily, with extensions to the existing planned periods happening in each round. The present contract period appears to be turning into the longest so far, as a result of companies' bargaining regarding the financing of satellite broadcasting. In this and in the rather secretive way in which the IBA works, the present system is not without its problems, though it has demonstrated its workability.

Notes on the literature

The basic idea of franchising as an alternative to regulation seems to have been around for a remarkably long time; for some historical background and useful discussion of the concept see Schmalensee (1979, ch. 5). The major modern theoretical impetus starts with Demsetz (1968) and also involves Posner (1974). An extensive critical treatment is given in Williamson (1976), whilst an interesting sidelight is cast on the subject by Klein et al. (1978), and Goldberg (1977) has a useful discussion. In addition to Williamson's cable TV case study, some useful material appears in *Public Money*, June 1983. The particular case of cable is pursued in the UK context by Veljanovski and Bishop (1983) and Waterson (1984b). For more on the early experience of independent television franchises, see Sendall (1982).

7

Privatization, Liberalization and Deregulation: Theory and Empirics

In examining state control, rate regulation and bidding schemes in the previous three chapters, we have found that none offers a general solution to the control of natural monopoly. This is by no means an idiosyncratic conclusion, for several countries have recently indulged in experimentation with the structure of such industries, presumably because they feel these structures fall some way short of ideal. Nevertheless, saying that particular controls do not work, or do not work well in some cases, does not imply that such controls are useless. It does imply, however, that we should examine the ways in which control may be loosened and, if possible, discern whether the effects are beneficial on balance. This is what I shall attempt to do in this chapter.

Experimentation with the loosening of control has essentially taken three forms, namely privatization, liberalization and deregulation, terms defined in the following section. These in turn lead to three questions that require answering. In pursuit of partial answers, I shall examine some cross-sectional empirical analyses and also a couple of case studies in later sections of the chapter. Sections 7.2, 7.3 and 7.4 deal with privatization, liberalization and deregulation, respectively.

7.1 Methods of loosening control

The terms privatization, liberalization and deregulation are often mixed up, or are not clearly defined. For example, Redwood and Hatch (1982) note that 'The word privatisation has become a portmanteau word covering a wide variety of different policies currently being pursued toward the nationalised industries . . .' (p. 121). I aim to provide definitions that attempt to clear distinctions, though no doubt others will disagree on semantic details.

Privatization or denationalization means a change in ownership from public to private. Privatization may be partial or full, so that some activities of the former company may be hived off (as with British Rail's hotels), the company may be forced to contract out some of its previously in-house activities (e.g. laundry or catering) or some or even the whole of the company's equity may be sold.

Liberalization means relaxing or abolishing restraints on entry into some of the areas previously the statutory or customary province of the monopoly incumbent. For example, the telephone equipment markets in many countries are now liberalized despite telephone operations still being carried out by one concern, often state-owned. I will tend to use the term for partial, rather than total freedoms to enter (unlike some other writers).

Deregulation means the removal or substantial diminution of the regulations by which the firm or firms in an industry are governed. This might mean the removal of price controls on a natural monopoly, which could nevertheless remain a natural monopoly barred to entry. If the regulations relate to entry or the qualities required of entrants (e.g. regarding safety), then deregulation is in some ways akin to liberalization. However, they are conceptually separate. A market may be liberalized without any regulations on standards being removed, whilst markets in which there is already competition (e.g. the supply of taxi services) might be deregulated. The point is that regulation normally covers much more than restrictions on entry, and essentially relates to core rather than peripheral activities.

This discussion points to an important problem we shall encounter in separating out the effects of particular actions. It is commonly the case that structural experiments take the form not of pure privatization, or whatever, but of a combination of two or three of the concepts as defined above. (This is, of course, the source of confusion in the definitions.) I shall nevertheless proceed below first by discussing the circumstances under which each of the pure policy instruments looks promising.

In the case of a natural monopoly, privatization will be beneficial or detrimental in its effects according to whether the controls on a publicly owned monopoly are socially superior to those on a privately owned one. This is essentially a comparative institutional question rather than one amenable to a priori analysis. For example, there may be greater incentives to productive efficiency in the private firm than the public if the 'market' for political control operates weakly. But there may be greater incentives to socially efficient pricing in the publicly owned firm, particularly if managers in the private sector are rewarded for producing high profits and as a result are encouraged to engage in anti-competitive behaviour. I shall not rehearse the arguments further here, since they have been covered already in chapters 3 and 4.

Liberalization is likely to be most beneficial when technical change or demand conditions have turned what was once a natural monopoly into an industry where parts at least would benefit from substantial competition. For example, when telephone systems were small in scale and standards were rudimentary and various, it probably made sense for the service provider also to provide instruments, or at least to monitor closely the provision of them. Now that demand has increased so much and technical change has made for a tremendous diversity in what it is useful to put on the end of a telephone line, liberalization of the equipment market makes a great deal of sense. Similarly, when the normal approach to a port for a sea crossing was made by rail, it was far more appropriate for the rail and the ferry service to be operated by the same firm than it is now.

One feature of regulation which has already been commented on in earlier chapters is that it tends to take on a momentum of its own. Two problems which can arise are that (*a*) the area of operations which is regulated, or the nature of regulation which is employed, has changed somewhat from the original intention and (*b*) technical and/or taste changes have rendered the scope or nature of regulation irrelevant. To give two examples: regulation of the UK bus and coach industries was originally intended to focus on matters of public safety, whereas it turned into tight control over route allocation and pricing (Glaister and Mulley, 1983); close regulatory control of prices would not be appropriate in the present-day canal industry.

This second example points to a difference between deregulation and liberalization. More entry is not required into canal services, so that liberalization would be to no avail and would not influence pricing, whereas price regulation is inappropriate because there is little monopoly power.[1] Economic regulation, as was stated earlier, normally covers both entry and prices. In some cases competition can be beneficial, in others increased contestability (e.g. through franchising) may be socially desirable, whereas in still others again, regulation, possibly coupled with controls on entry, remains optimal, despite changing circumstances. Notice also that privatization, of itself, implies nothing about the desirability or otherwise of deregulation.

These three policies, privatization, liberalization and deregulation, lead naturally to three empirical questions of some importance:

[1]An absence of substantial monopoly power is often equated with demand being relatively elastic, which is probably untrue for canals. However, I believe this argument is not definitive, for two reasons. First, the possible implication that monopoly is associated with demand being (absolutely) inelastic is false, as elementary textbooks demonstrate. Secondly, if demand in one case is relatively inelastic, this does not necessarily imply anything about the size of monopoly welfare loss relative to other relevant magnitudes, for example total surplus created by the product. Indeed, in the case of linear demand, the fraction (monopoly welfare loss/total surplus) is a constant independent of demand elasticity (Cable et al., 1982). Of course, if demand is relatively inelastic, as might be the case with canals, the impact on certain people may be large.

1   Is one form of ownership better than another *in natural monopoly industries*?
2   Has entry occurred in liberalized markets, and does it appear to have been worthwhile?
3   Does deregulation prove beneficial or, to put it another way, do the regulatory devices employed actually seem to have an economic rationale?

The remainder of this chapter is devoted to an examination of these questions, partly by means of surveys of empirical studies, partly through use of case study material but with a backcloth of theory. In each case some care needs to be taken in making the comparison of like with like, and true comparisons are not always available.

7.2   Public versus private monopolies

There have been many comparative studies of public with private firms, some of which are essentially irrelevant because those involved are not in monopoly or near-monopoly positions. The comparisons may be divided into those between industries in which there is one natural incumbent normally associated with priced output (e.g. utilities), and those where contracts or franchises are awarded by competitive tender (e.g. cleansing and refuse), where there is normally no separate charge. In the case of the former they can be either cost/(total) factor productivity or pricing studies.

What is ideally required for all such comparisons is a sample of firms that are alike in all respects save their ownership structure. In general this is not available and studies have plumped either for very small sample pairwise comparisons or, more commonly, larger sample comparisons using regression analysis with control variables. The point is that if, for example, scale or factor prices vary, then the comparison will normally be biased. Suppose that we wish to compare refuse collection in city X with collection in city Y and suppose, for the sake of argument, that there are some economies of scale in refuse collection — a reasonable presumption. The city which is more optimally sized from the point of view of the available scale economies is inherently more likely to have lower costs. Population density also has a part to play. Equally, if we were to compare electricity generation costs between two cities, it would be important to take account of relative city sizes and any differences in fuel costs. Assuming factor prices are exogenous (i.e. they do not contain monopoly rent elements) and assuming locations are given, it must be correct to take account of every other source of difference before making the comparison between public and private. As a corollary, crude comparisons of the 'costs slashed by 40 per cent on going private' type are nonsensical if the only source of differential costs is, say, differential wages (in the sense of a pure transfer) or reduced service.

Of course, the prevailing political and economic climate has an influence on what organizational forms actually exist at any one time. For reasons of its size and diversity, the present-day United Sates tends to throw up rather more examples of differing organizational structures in industries such as electricity generation than, say, the UK, though at various times in the past in the UK there has been experimentation with organizational form. These biases will, naturally, be reflected in the present review.

The preliminaries aside, let us proceed to discuss cost studies. The electricity supply industry has proved a fruitful source of data. Here the studies have in recent years become rather sophisticated, with Pescatrice and Trapani (1980), for instance, employing a translog cost function approach and also taking account of different vintages of generating equipment, whilst Foreman-Peck and Waterson (1985) (hereafter F-P/W) capture three different dimensions of output in their work. The basic idea in both cases is that generating costs are a function of output level and type, input factor prices, the level of technology and the form of ownership, thus:

$$C = C(Y, W, T, D)$$

where Y refers to a vector of output (in F-P/W's case units generated, maximum load and length of production time) constructed in such a way as to allow scale effects, W is a vector of factor prices (e.g. labour, capital and fuel prices), T is the level of technology and D is a (or a vector of) ownership-type dummy variables. Pescatrice and Trapani's sample is of recent US experience, incorporating both municipally and privately owned utilities, whereas F-P/W's sample refers to UK municipal and private firms in 1937.

Speaking broadly, the results of these studies accord with intuition — there are scale economies up to a substantial output in electricity generation, and factor prices are important, implying that substitution possibilities are available, though they would probably involve changing plant size at the same time; fuel price in particular is an important element in costs. In Pescatrice and Trapani's study, costs were if anything lower in publicly owned firms, all other things equal. In F-P/W, the publicly owned firms were on average less efficient, though this was due to a longer 'tail' of inefficient smaller firms, and the larger ones 'selected' by the Central Electricity Board (as it was then called) for supply to the national grid were equally as efficient as the private ones.

Similar types of studies to these two have been made by Caves and Christensen (1980) on Canadian Railroads (using a total factor productivity approach) and more recently by Millward and Ward (1987) on town gas supply in the UK at the turn of the century. In both cases these were similarly careful attempts to include sufficient control variables to compare like with like. Both conclude with essentially neutral effects; once these other factors are accounted for there seems little difference statistically between ownership types, though in both cases, for separate reasons, there is weak evidence in favour of the public firms being more efficient.

Additional studies of electricity generation, and also water provision, along the lines described above are reported in Borcherdling et al. (1982) and Yarrow (1986). These authors present a mixed picture, with Yarrow concluding narrowly in favour of higher public-firm efficiency and Borcherdling's group reaching the opposite conclusion. It appears on balance that there may be no substantial advantage to one organizational form or another. Other surveys reinforce this conclusion. It might also, incidentally, receive implicit support from the fact that although the Energy Act 1983 has permitted private firms in the UK to supply electricity to the national grid on a continuing basis, and at least two have investigated the possibility, nevertheless firms have not so far commenced supply. (On this point, however, see also Hammond et al., 1986.)

Analyses of differences of pricing structures of otherwise similar private and public utilities have also been performed, again focusing on electricity in the United States. Two important studies (Peltzman, 1971; de Alessi, 1977) find that tariffs in publicly owned concerns less closely reflect the costs of the particular customers charged than they do in privately owned firms. Since electricity is a non-storable product where peak costs are a significant proportion of total costs, it is efficient to have tariffs reflect this, as well as to design them so as to even out peaks. In this sense, both studies find the private companies more efficient. However, there is evidence, albeit in some cases historic (Baker, 1915), that private electricity companies charge relatively high prices compared with publicly owned ones. Moreover, as Yarrow (1986) points out, the tariff structures in the present-day US electricity industry are much less sophisticated than those in the state-owned UK and French industries, and US utilities have been much less inclined to impose time-of-day pricing (Hausman and Neufeld, 1984) than have the UK and French concerns.

Now let us turn to a consideration of the tendering cases. Here Borcherdling et al. (1982), Millward (1982) and Yarrow (1986) are all in agreement that in areas such as refuse collection and cleansing services, the available evidence points to privately owned firms being cheaper on average than municipal operations by a significant amount. Again, the approach adopted in empirical studies commonly is to take a sample of operations, some publicly and some privately run, and control as far as possible for

factors which might make for differences not due to efficiency, but which
influence costs. Thus in refuse collection, frequency and other features
of service, population density, placing of dispersal sites and so on, are
all relevant. It appears from these studies that, by and large, franchising
of simple, easily specified tasks, works (as the theory discussed in chapter
6 suggests).

The papers surveyed in the three articles cited in the previous paragraph
focus again upon the North American environment. Recently, however,
as a result of changes, the UK has thrown up substantial evidence of the
effects of competitive tendering for franchises to clean, launder for and
collect refuse from local authority, National Health Service and Ministry
of Defence establishments. Hartley and Huby (1986) and Domberger et
al. (1986) have studied some of the early effects.

On the basis of their postal survey, Hartley and Huby conclude that 'the
percentage saving from competitive tendering would average 26 per cent
per annum' (p. 292) though there was a wide variance in this, and in some
cases extra costs would be incurred by the authority. It is important to
note, however, that these are not true like-with-like comparisons. Wage
costs and other service conditions under outside operators were normally
lower. There is also a suggestion that complaints about the service provided by outside contractors are running at rather high levels, and indeed,
the TUC (1984) has collected an impressive dossier of contractors' failures.
Yet the rather carefully normalized (regression) analysis of Domberger
et al. also suggests that the experience has resulted in an overall improvement in efficiency, with real costs lower by around 20 per cent. Real costs
fell by a significant amount whether outside firms or the internal applicants
received the contract,[2] indicating substantial cost savings made as a result
merely of the introduction of tendering — liberalization rather than privatization effects?

Apart from the studies referred to above, Pryke has made analyses of
state-owned concerns in the UK (e.g. 1981). These seek to draw more
general comparisons between the state firms and the private sector, but
they also include non-monopoly firms such as British Leyland, and the
comparison is much less clearly of like with like. The emphasis is more
on the failures of the state firms than on a comparative institutional approach,
since private concerns, as Pryke acknowledges, are by no means perfect.
Hence, although interesting, these studies are less relevant to the present
purpose.

---

[2]In some cases, it appears, internal applicants were discriminated against in awarding
contracts.

Finally, a perhaps rather mundane, but nevertheless important point, changing a firm from a publicly to a privately owned concern is an expensive business. The privatization of British Telecom is said to have cost about £152 million in marketing, underwriting commissions, fees to advisers and so on, and British Gas about £164 million, of which marketing costs amounted to £41 million, or about £9 per eventual shareholder. In the case of BT, the costs were about 4 per cent of total valuation; with British Gas around half that, though it is reported[3] that 4 per cent, £220 million, has been set aside for the incentives, in the form of reduced bills, to small shareholders. To these figures must be added the social welfare losses involved in the transfer of money from the state (i.e. UK citizens) to those who obtained shares, which rose to a substantial premium in the case of BT.[4] The point here is not to boggle at the magnitudes involved, but rather to note that such privatization actions should not lightly be undertaken since a minor difference in efficiency would quickly be wiped out by the transaction costs involved.

7.3 The effects of liberalizing entry

It should be recalled that we are defining liberalization as the permitting of entry into essentially peripheral areas of operation: entry into core areas is discussed in the following section. Nevertheless, it would be difficult to draw a clear dividing line between core and peripheral areas, and it is naturally the case that the effects of entry generally are relevant both to this section and the next. My plan in this section is to discuss the effects of entry generally, from both theoretical and empirical standpoints, and then to examine a specific case.

The impact of entry generally

In the standard models of perfect competition, entry is an important and beneficial force. If price remains above average cost, then in the long run entry occurs, and does so until price is equated with average, as well as

---

[3]The figures come from newspaper reports in *The Times* and *The Financial Times* of 13 December 1986 concerning Parliamentary written answers.

[4]This amount is obviously less than the amount of the transfer itself, but that was perhaps a third of the asset valuation. The point may obviously be made that the costs are once-for-all, whilst the benefits continue. However the widely respected 'efficient markets hypothesis' would suggest that the best estimate of the stock market's valuation of the prospective benefits is provided by the share valuation of the company concerned. Hence our comparisons are with that figure.

marginal, cost. Easy entry is thus one of the cornerstones of competitive analysis. Where there is not perfect competition, entry is no longer necessarily easy. But as Bain (1956) and many others since have pointed out, potential as well as actual entry is an important behaviour-modifying force. The 'perfect contestability' view is that potential competition is in many ways superior to actual entry.[5] Indeed, actual entry may in some circumstances be wasteful, as we saw in chapter 2. The reason appears to be connected with the presence of fixed costs and the wasteful duplication of these costs. This theoretical perspective can be sharpened by drawing on the recent analysis of Mankiw and Whinston (1986), which itself draws insights from Spence (1976) and others.

Mankiw and Whinston identify two fundamental forces acting in opposite directions on the number of entrants, one due to what they dub a 'business-stealing effect', the other arising through product heterogeneity. When entry occurs, the new firm gains sales partly from new customers and partly through 'stealing' former customers of established firms. Both contribute to profits of the entrant, but the entrant does not of course take into account the losses engendered for others, though it would be socially optimal to do so. This is a force leading towards excessive entry, from a societal viewpoint. However, if there is product differentiation/diversity, another factor comes into play. A firm introducing a product is unable to capture all of the surplus created as a result of the increased product variety. As Spence (1976) pointed out, this is a conservative force, leading by itself to too few products being produced. There is also a further complicating factor, the integer constraint. Free entry will not in fact lead to zero profits except by chance, because each entrant incurs a lumpy fixed cost element of expenditure.

As a result of these factors, assuming that aggregate output rises with the number of firms, but that output per firm falls, Mankiw and Whinston show that the free entry equilibrium number of firms is never less than the socially optimal number minus one but may be many more — a tendency in general towards excessive entry. Yet if entry increases variety and, thereby, social welfare, the tendency to excessive entry need not persist. Indeed, under one formulation, Mankiw and Whinston find that the equilibrium number of firms is always less than the optimum number.

In short, both the forces thought intuitively to be important influences are shown to have their expected effects, and in consequence there may be either too many or too few firms in the industry as a result of free entry.

Mankiw and Whinston also show that, when set-up costs become small,

---

[5]Some writers have, rather ahistorically, identified Bain's view as one of 'imperfect contestability'.

the free entry number of firms need not approach the optimal number. Moreover, it is not even true in every case that the welfare loss arising in a model where firms are assumed to enter until the next entrant would not be profitable, becomes small as fixed costs shrink. However if, as the number of entrants becomes large, firms act as price-takers, then the social welfare loss approaches zero as fixed costs approach zero. This result shows on what fragile foundations rests the idea that free entry is socially desirable. In many cases, it seems, making entry easier need not improve the social welfare position of the industry, particularly if fixed costs are relatively high and there are tendencies towards cartelization of the industry.

Nevertheless, *replacement* entry as opposed to accrual entry is always desirable, if we assume that the replacement is merely a more efficient version of the firm it replaces. Here other firms suffer rather less business stealing, but in any case the number of fixed cost lumps does not increase, therefore no additional social costs are created,[6] so the net effect is purely beneficial. The implicit assumption behind the 'business stealing' argument presented above is that all established firms suffer but none is driven out of business — the cake is sliced more thinly — whereas it may quite commonly be the case that the weaker firms suffer proportionately more due to efficient new entry and possibly are driven out. Making allowance for this increases the set of circumstances under which entry is definitely desirable.

This brings us to empirics. There have been many studies of the determinants of entry, but fewer on the effects. Perhaps inevitably, given the differing nature of the phenomena, those on the effects tend to be less analytical in content. For instance, there is usually no attempt to evaluate any *losses* due to entry, nor thus to compare these rigorously with benefits such as price falls; still less to evaluate the benefits of increased variety. All these factors are important in the overall assessment, but they are undoubtedly difficult to measure. Even in the case of price changes, the counterfactual may not be straightforward, as can be noted in the context of a specific example below.

It may perhaps be possible to come to some crude generalizations regarding the effects of entry in practice. First, the immediate effect is usually either primarily an aggressive price response, or an enforced cutback in supply, or possibly a nonprice (e.g. advertising) strategy. One might consider, as examples, the impact of Laker Airways on the transatlantic airline scene, the reaction to Japanese entry into the UK colour television market and (a rather older case) the domestic washing machine suppliers' response

---

[6]Though, of course, there may be some sunk cost element associated with the exit.

to Rolls Razor. In some cases, a mixture of responses is employed, see, for example, Shaw (1974), regarding established petroleum companies' attempts to limit the incursion of firms such as Continental (suppliers of 'Jet'). Some of these effects are clearly desirable — the Laker case introduced essentially new traffic, but aided the reduction in price for some established traffic. Other examples are less clearly so, particularly when they involve mutually self-cancelling advertising campaigns and the like.

The second effect that entry has, commonly, is to sharpen the competitive position of the established firms. If entry has been brought about through an essentially different product (e.g. the washing machine example, also Japanese cars), then developing a response can take some time, maybe up to five years. In the meantime, there may have been further entry.

A third common effect is that of retrenchment by the established firm(s), often accompanied by rises in prices, as the fight for market share is eased. Sometimes the entrant will have been driven out (as with Rolls Razor and Laker), on other occasions, a form of accommodation will have been reached (Japanese cars and televisions). The end product will often look rather different (e.g. potato crisps after Golden Wonder's entry), arguably superior. But any general evaluation of the effects must be rather difficult. In particular, evaluation in some cases would have to be against the benchmark of the (limited) discipline imposed by the threat of potential entry. It is perhaps best to turn directly to a specific case of liberalizing entry, though some of the points above will recur in section 7.4.

Entry into the telecommunications customer premise equipment (CPE) market

In many countries, as a part of the organization of telecommunications as a regulated or state-owned industry, the telecoms operator has also been allowed to control closely what the customer puts on the end of the telephone line. Looked at from one point of view, this might seem absurd; it would be difficult to imagine the electricity supplier or the gas company dictating what applicances you could use, let alone insisting that you buy all such appliances from them.

However, matters are not quite this straightforward. The electricity company will refuse to connect you if in its judgement your wiring is dangerous, and the gas company prevents you from connecting certain types of appliance which would have a deleterious effect upon neighbouring gas supplies. Moreover, the issue is slightly more complex in the case of telephones. In principle, not only might you harm yourself (which might reflect badly upon the company), or harm company employees, but the equipment you connect might also impair other people's communications with you (called second party harm), or even other network users (third party harm).

In reality then, the issues regarding CPE are not related to questions of natural monopoly, but rather to standards of safety and of interconnection. It is perhaps unlikely that whatever you do will seriously disadvantage the telephone company, but the possibility arguably should be guarded against. The question then is whether the company or some separate standard-setting body should oversee this. Implicitly, it was often assumed that the company knew best, but this allowed companies to take control of equipment sales. The pendulum has now swung in the direction of separate standard-setting agencies.

In some countries the equipment market has been liberalized for some time. For example in Japan the CPE market (beyond the first telephone set) was opened in 1953 to firms apart from the national carrier NTT, and the West German market has been to some extent liberalized since early this century. However, major CPE markets such as the United States, the UK and much of the rest of Western Europe have been in telecom company hands until comparatively recently and have been relinquished rather reluctantly.

In the United States liberalization started with such extraordinary events such as the 'Hush-a-Phone' decision, whereby in 1956 it was finally decided that consumers could use plastic sound-muffling devices on their telephones without payment of an additional tariff. More important was the 'Carterphone' ruling in 1968 which allowed subscribers to choose all appliances apart from the first. Since then, the Federal Communications Commission has developed a programme of liberalization subject to minimal standards.

The effects of the resultant entry of non-company affiliated suppliers into the CPE market seem very largely to have been beneficial. In the area of telephone instruments, sales have increased greatly, boosted enormously in 1984 by sales of equipment currently in place but leased by the user. (This is an option unavailable in the UK.) New telephones are widely available from a number of manufacturers at prices which have held roughly constant but which reflect increasingly 'feature-packed' instruments. Many of these are inexpensive imports from Japan and other Far Eastern countries.

In the Private Branch Exchange (PBX, sometimes PABX) market, there has been tremendous market growth, perhaps 15 per cent per year, and average price per line has dropped dramatically in money terms, let alone real terms, perhaps halving since the early 1980s (United States Department of Commerce, 1985). Interestingly, Northern Telecom, a non-(US) affiliated Canadian manufacturer, was most likely the largest supplier of PBXs in 1984 (according to the same source) and over a five-year period, AT & T's market share fell from 80 to 25 per cent (Müller, 1986), though both it and Rolm (an IBM subsidiary) had healthy market shares. Concentration is rather higher in PBXs than in simple instruments. The intermediate 'key systems' market (small exchanges) is dominated to a greater extent by AT & T, but here again prices have fallen.

In the UK the CPE market was almost entirely closed to suppliers other than British Telecom until the passing of the Telecommunications Act 1981, which permitted the attachment of privately owned equipment. Facilitating this was the introduction of a new plug and socket system in 1982, although BT currently has, and shows no signs of relinquishing, the sole right to convert householders to this system. Initially also, BT was the body which evaluated and approved all supplier equipment, though under the 1984 Telecommunications Act, a new authority, the British Approvals Board for Telecommunications, will perform this function.

As a result of these changes, the market in telephone handsets, answering machines etc., has changed very considerably. Large numbers of handsets have been approved (e.g. 130 models in the last nine months of 1985; see Carsberg, 1986) and they are retailed from a variety of outlets. As in the United States, Far Eastern products have penetrated the market heavily. Yet so far only one quarter of households are in this market (Foreman-Peck and Manning, 1986) since the others still have no socket conversion and British Telecom's charges for carrying out the conversion are, arguably, at artificially high levels. Once converted, purchase of a telephone (from BT or elsewhere) is substantially cheaper than rental of one from BT.

The market in PBXs has changed rather less, though on one level it seems to have been in a state of considerable activity. Upon liberalization, BT persuaded 40 per cent of PBX customers to replace their equipment (Foreman-Peck and Manning, 1986), and this considerable turnover has continued, so that a *Financial Times* survey in 1985 (17 May 1985) reported that 70 per cent of exchanges had been replaced within that four-year period.

However, BT appears to have deliberately adopted an aggressive marketing strategy (Müller, 1986) in order to pre-empt moves into the market by competitors, helped of course by its knowledge of customers' current installations. As a result, equipment suppliers and Mercury, the newly licensed network operator, have found it relatively difficult to move into the PBX market in a big way. Between 1981 and 1984, according to Gist and Meadowcroft (1986), BT *increased* its PBX market share from 65 to 74 per cent. More generally, one effect of liberalization has been that the traditional UK equipment suppliers have been squeezed in the process, not least because their previously cosy relationship with BT has been broken. This process has been greatly aided by BT's merger (subject to restrictions) with a powerful 'upstart' equipment manufacturer, Mitel. This company was an important supplier to the independents.

On balance, then, it appears that liberalization has been associated with substantial changes in the CPE markets. Nevertheless, it might justifiably be objected that much of the evidence is rather impressionistic. There is still a paucity of comparative work focusing upon the changes in the CPE market, for instance between (*a*) recently liberalized markets, (*b*) sometime liberalized markets and (*c*) unliberalized markets.

This is an important gap in our knowledge, because it seems most likely that technological change would have brought about benefits to consumers in the absence of liberalization. In the face of falling costs a monopolist may be expected to reduce prices, and there are several sets of circumstances under which in theory a monopoly will set quality embedded in a unit of product at the same level as would a competitive industry structure (see Saving, 1982). Hence the expected direction of the effects observed would have been the same in the absence of liberalization. That said, at least in the case of simple items of equipment, fixed costs would probably be low and suppliers' behaviour may approach price-taking, so that on earlier arguments one would expect the effect of introducing competition in the market to be beneficial to society as a whole. This does not, however, rule out possibly severe adverse effects on domestic producers.

7.4 The effects of deregulation

Deregulation is almost bound to have a variety of effects, since regulation itself may or may not provide a tight constraint. The approach followed here is again to focus largely on a specific example, following some general and some theoretical remarks, rather than to attempt a general review. This is bound to be selective, but the trend to deregulation, like the trend to liberalization, is relatively new, so that a general review would inevitably be seriously incomplete.

At the outset, it is relevant briefly to recall some of the facets and effects of regulation itself. First, regulation usually imposes some standards of service, it often controls entry and also often controls price or rate of return. Secondly, presumably there must have been some pressing reason for regulation initially, but this does not mean that the current structure of regulation has a logical form. Regulation often gains a momentum of its own (see chapter 1) as the regulators try to ensure their position is entrenched (or, perhaps we should say, important), so the standards demanded might be unnecessarily high, or the entry requirements unnecessarily strict, or whatever.

Removal of regulation, then, may well reduce costs by relaxing regulatory requirements or by removing cost-increasing effects (e.g. the Averch–Johnson effect; for an empirical analysis, see e.g. Nelson and Wohar, 1983).

It is likely to increase the contestability of the market as controls on entry and other sundry requirements are dropped. It may result in entry (on which see the previous section). But the effects on prices arguably are uncertain. If, due to deregulation, costs are reduced by some small amount but the firm (or firms) involved is able to increase the price−cost margin as a result of relaxed controls, prices could rise. On some arguments this is unlikely given the increased contestability, but there is the question of what effect increased contestability has. An increase in competition taken by itself would reduce price−cost margins, but contestability need not follow the same limit process. This important issue is discussed below.

Effects of increased contestability

Realistically, perfect contestability can be considered only to be a benchmark, not a practical state of affairs. In the same way, perfect competition is a benchmark. However, perfect competition gains considerably in relevance through the fact that many limit theorems can be shown to apply. Specifically, as an industry becomes more nearly perfectly competitive in structure, it also becomes more competitive in behaviour. The question is whether such limit results hold for perfect contestability, to which the answer is that to some extent they do, but in other respects they do not, as I shall illustrate. I shall also present some experimental evidence which bears on the question.

To look at the limiting relationship, consider the following simple framework (similar to Vickers and Yarrow, 1985, and Schwartz, 1986), illustrated in figure 7.1. There is an incumbent in the industry in question, and a lag of length E between the time at which an entrant makes a decision to enter, and successful entry taking place. If entry involves a price below that currently available from the incumbent, all customers switch to the entrant, until such time as the incumbent is able to respond by changing price (Bertrand−Nash behaviour). To respond takes a time T from the time of entry. The effect of the incumbent's response, we shall assume, is that both firms remain in production, selling at a price p_c which implies breakeven or normal profits. Of course, we must incorporate

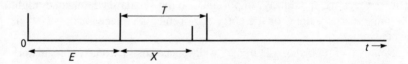

Figure 7.1 Contestability and entry lags

some form of scale economies, say through fixed costs, and we assume that if the firm exits before a time X has elapsed after entry, none (for simplicity) of these are recoverable, whereas if exit has not taken place by time X, the costs are recovered. This can be thought of as a simple representation of the degree to which costs are sunk. The speed of cost recovery naturally depends upon price, and we assume $X = X(p)$; $X' < 0$, $X_c = X(p_c)$.

Within this framework, perfect contestability can be characterized as: $X_c = 0$, $T > 0$, E small. Hit and run entry is both (marginally) profitable and feasible, and takes place fairly quickly, so the incumbent must at most break even. This result extends to the case where $T > X_c > 0$, at least in part. Here there is no point in deterring entry, because it will always be profitable, but the incumbent equally has no incentive not to charge monopoly price over period E.[7]

Rather more radical things happen if $X_c \geq 0$ but $T = 0$ (and a fortiori, if $T < 0$, which is feasible). It is then never worthwhile for entry to take place, even if monopoly price is set by the incumbent. Thus there is a fairly abrupt change in the character of the game when T changes between zero (or negative) and positive. A very quick price response by the established firm is a potent deterrent to potential competition, despite high current industry profitability. Indeed, it may be considered that incumbents can commonly be fairly flexible about price responses, so that they can observe the entrant building up to capacity and then cut price quickly to exclude the entrant from the market. Hence this is an empirically relevant case.

Finally, we have the situation where $X_c > T > 0$. Here, there will be some price, $p_L > p_c$ above which $X(p_L) \leq T$. Entry deterrence can be achieved by setting price p_L. But the important point is that where T is rather small, p_L may be substantially above p_c even if X_c is small. Indeed, if retaliation time is fairly short, entry might not be profitable even where the incumbent is currently setting monopoly price. Again we see the crucial importance of the precise assumptions made regarding T and X. Since we cannot imagine in practice that $X_c = 0$, the results suggest that in some highly (though not perfectly) contestable industries, the incumbent may in fact be able to earn high profits. Moreover, if $T = 0$, making the market seemingly more contestable by means of a reduction in X_c has no effect upon performance in the industry — it does not reduce monopoly power. This is relevant, for example, to policies designed to reduce the extent to which costs are sunk.

---

[7]Incidentally, one might characterize the attempt to design an ideal bidding scheme as an attempt to create a market environment where $X_c \simeq T$ and E is very small.

In sum, the most potent policy to improve performance is to increase *T* by artificial means, for example by requiring incumbents to set prices on a long-term basis. Reducing sunk cost elements may or may not improve performance.

Experimental evidence that bears on this matter has begun to accumulate (see Coursey et al., 1984; Harrison and McKee, 1985, for example). These experiments do not relate to direct experience but rather to laboratory-style behaviour. The typical arrangement is where two players acting as sellers independently post price offers on computer screens, based upon which 'buyers' make their purchases. Reality is induced by paying the participants in amounts related directly to their performance.

As a broad generalization, these studies confirm the rather mixed conclusions we have already reached. To start with something concrete, when experimental conditions are as closely in line with the theoretical requirements for perfect contestability as can be obtained, then the results essentially accord with theoretical predictions. But this finding, whilst interesting in its own right, is not relevant to our present concern, which is to investigate how closely results approach predictions when moderate changes in the assumptions away from those associated with perfect contestability are maintained.

It must next be said that when the conditions are varied in almost any way from the theoretical requirements for perfect contestability, the results no longer accord with the 'strong' form of contestability — that price equals average cost (at the lowest intersection point). Recall that the theory requires the incumbent to post prices before the potential entrants do so (so that $T > 0$). Thus, simultaneous independent posting of prices goes against the theory (as Harrison and McKee admit). Simultaneous posting and no sunk costs leads to a weak form of contestability — that prices are nearer to competitive or average cost prices than to monopoly prices — rather than the strong form being accepted. But there is a potentially serious criticism of this rendering of the theory, namely that one is actually assessing duopoly interaction here rather than anything else (see Schwartz, 1986).

Be that as it may, the more interesting extension of the model is that catering for sunk costs (Coursey et al., 1984). In this series of experiments the weak version of the contestable markets hypothesis holds up on average, but that average conceals considerable diversity. Two experiments were suggestive of tacit collusion between firms, and one exhibited a form of limit pricing behaviour, whilst five exhibited convergence towards competitive behaviour. In all these experiments, the period *E* (pre-entry) is significant, and within it the incumbent shows very little restraint, as might be expected from what was said earlier.

Harrison and McKee do not have sunk costs, but they do investigate

a variety of methods of control as alternatives to increasing market contestability. It is interesting, in the context of discussion in earlier chapters,
to note some of their conclusions. Specifically, a decentralized regulatory
incentive scheme (Loeb-Magat, see section 4.3) outperforms contestability,
as does a Vickrey franchising auction scheme. Thus it is implied that ideal
regulation, or alternatively franchising, can do more to induce a competitive
regime than does increased contestability. Of course, this abstracts from
all of the difficulties of regulation we adumbrated in chapter 5, also from
all the problems of franchising discussed in chapter 6. But it does bring
us very firmly back into the realm of comparative institutional analysis
concerning the appropriate control mechanism for natural monopoly. With
this background, let us turn now to a specific example, airline deregulation.

Deregulation of airlines in the United States

The extent of airline deregulation in the United States has been considerable.
When it was set up in 1938, the Civil Aviation Board (CAB) was empowered
in effect to control entry of new airlines, and entry into new routes, also
to control exit, to regulate fares, to award subsidies, to control mergers
and other intercarrier arrangements, and to oversee safety standards. This
last responsibility has for some time not been theirs, and all the other
activities have now either been discontinued or, in one or two cases (prin-
cipally mergers, also subsidies through a declining programme), have been
passed to the Department of Transportation. As a result of the Airline
Deregulation Act 1978, the CAB no longer exists. Entry restrictions were
substantially relaxed immediately, and since 1982 entry has been free to
all suitably qualified carriers. In 1983 all fare restrictions were abolished,
though these had been eased even in the run-up period to the Act, from
1976. Clearly, what has happened in the United States in the airline sphere
is much more far-reaching than the liberalization of the telephone CPE
market which formed our earlier example. So, what of the effects?

The first point to make is that deregulation has not been an unmitigated
disaster. In fact many commentators claim it as a considerable success.
Nevertheless, it is equally untrue that everyone, or even *every* airline
passenger, has benefited. Casual extrapolation from the effects of entry
into the London—New York route — substantially lower fares, cheap-and-
cheerful carriers, and so on — would be seriously misleading. In fact, what
the academic studies point to is a picture of considerable diversity. Some
classes of passenger have clearly lost out whilst others have gained. Hence
it cannot be claimed that the deregulated outcome is Pareto-superior to
the regulatory position. Moreover, it goes without saying that, since 'other
things' are never equal, disentangling the effects of deregulation from those

of extraneous phenomena such as cyclical movements in the economy is not straightforward. We will look at the impact of these effects, as recorded in secondary sources.

The most noticeable phenomenon has been an intensifying of the 'hub and spoke' network concept,[8] where airlines are each associated with an airport (the hub) to which most of its services fly, and from which passengers can obtain connections to a wide variety of other places. To Europeans used to what is known as 'interlining', that is, changing airlines in the course of a journey from, say, Newcastle to Brussels via Amsterdam, this may seem curious. Why are passengers so keen to travel on a single carrier's flights that it is efficient for each carrier to develop its own hub and spoke networks? The answer, it appears (see e.g. Carlton et al., 1980), is that by travelling with a single carrier, customers reduce the chances of missed connections, lost baggage etc. Since in the United States many airlines do not practise interlining, ticket purchase would also be more complex.

If we accept that there is a very strong preference for single carrier service, then the effects of increased hub and spoke operation are that far more timings can be offered to the client, although most of these will be relatively slow, since they involve transfer at a hub. As a consequence, one of the predicted effects of deregulation, a reduction in flight frequency, has not generally occurred; if anything, the opposite has happened. (Nevertheless some small communities have lost service altogether.) At the same time, there is an important difficulty in evaluating the effects of deregulation. As transport economists are well aware, there are different average 'values of time' involved in different activities, for example, time on the aeroplane compared with time in the airport waiting for a connection. In addition, the emerging time and frequency patterns are both distance and route-type sensitive. Thus measuring overall effects on convenience of the service becomes relatively complex.

That said, authoritative studies (e.g. Bailey et al., 1985; Morrison and Winston, 1986) agree that there has been no decline in overall convenience, if anything an improvement,[9] once the various factors are weighed together.

Fares present a clearer but still mixed picture. Again in contrast to some expectations, fares have not all fallen in real terms below projected fares under regulatory control. It appears that one distortionary effect of regulation was to make long distance flights expensive. Another was to enforce a

---

[8]Incidentally, this contrasts sharply with what appears to have happened following deregulation of express coach services in the UK, for example.

[9]Bailey et al.'s 1985 study has 1981, a slump year, as its endpoint, but the authors still find no convenience decline, on balance.

relatively inflexible system of fare-setting. Hence, as a result first of fare relaxation then of deregulation, discounted fares have increased in importance and variety, and there has been some rebalancing of fares making short haul relatively more expensive and long haul relatively cheaper. So some fares, particularly undiscounted fares between smallish places relatively close together, have risen. But discounted fares now cover a considerable proportion of passengers and discounts are commonly very high. Consequently, Morrison and Whinston calculate that full fares have risen on average in real terms, but they also find an average fall of more than 15 per cent in actual fares paid in real terms over their period.

An important consequence of the increased fare flexibility is that load factors have improved, particularly on long distance flights. The development of capacity-controlled fares on a flight-by-flight basis (i.e. allocations of specific but different numbers of cheap seats on different flights) has allowed full fare passengers a high probability of seat availability whilst helping to fill the planes. Again there are extraneous features which make definitive statements difficult — cyclical factors obviously have an impact, but so do things such as the forced grounding of DC10s for a period. Nevertheless, since deregulation, load factors appear to have been at historically high levels.

Load factor improvements obviously contribute to greater productivity. Other sources of productivity gains since deregulation have included increased employee utilization as a result of renegotiated flight crew contracts. Local airlines seem to have been particularly successful in their efforts to increase employee productivity. Hence, paradoxically, despite the well-publicised bankruptcies, the financial health of airlines arguably is better than it would have been under regulation.

To summarize, plausible arguments and analyses indicate that though some people have suffered from deregulation, on balance the effects are positive. In their attempt at quantification, Morrison and Winston suggest benefits to travellers (mainly accruing to business travellers) of $5.7 billion annually, and to the airline industry, $2.5 billion. In addition, abolishing the CAB has saved $100 million in direct costs. Yet we must go some way to correcting this over-rosy picture of deregulation.

First, the evidence is against the proposition that regulation (perversely) succeeded in completely stultifying the industry. In fact, between 1949 and 1969 air fares fell significantly in real (and even slightly in nominal) terms, as Bailey et al. acknowledge. Air traffic increased a great deal, and the industry flourished. Hence the implicit charge against the regulators must be that they allowed insufficient flexibility in pricing and routeing into the system.

Secondly, it is clear that deregulation has resulted in neither a perfectly competitive nor even a perfectly contestable market for air travel. The former may be discounted on the basis of widespread price discrimination far beyond that expected by reference to differences in costs. As regards the other possibility, price discrimination is compatible with Ramsey pricing and so may be consistent with perfect contestability. But, despite high mobility of aircraft, other sunk costs facing entrants, such as consumer preferences, the requirement for advertising and other start-up costs etc., may be substantial (see Baumol and Willig, 1986). Moreover, there is clear evidence that incumbents' prices are not 'sticky'. Hence the theoretical requirements for perfect contestability are not met. The result, both Bailey et al. and Morrison and Winston agree, is that industry behaviour is (at best) imperfectly contestable. Bailey et al. find empirically that industry structure is not endogenous, as contestability would predict, but is exogenously determined, and also that the Herfindahl index of concentration (a common summary statistic of market power) is a significant explainer of price. As a result, their estimates suggest that duopoly market fares are lower than monopoly fares by 6 per cent and four-firm market fares are lower than monopoly by 11 per cent, other things being equal. Both this and their additional results are in line with Morrison and Winston's conclusion that 'the largest carriers tend to determine market conditions, while the smaller carriers and potential entrants have an important influence on the super-majors' actions . . .' (p. 64). Baumol and Willig (1986) and Schwartz (1986) concur.

Thirdly, we must remember that some additional adverse factors must be put into the balance. Planes are now more crowded, seats are more densely packed into the plane and inflight service is inferior. All these things have an implicit valuation, albeit small. More importantly, there are increased worries over safety as a result of longer crew hours, and in some cases, inadequately trained cabin crew. The hub and spoke system exacerbates safety problems since it increases the number of landings and takeoffs and the amount of circling around airports.

Finally, and most importantly, it is still rather early in the post-deregulatory time frame for final conclusions to emerge. The industry could still be in a state of disequilibrium. It is unclear whether deregulation will lead to a once-for-all change (improvement?) in circumstances, a continuous improvement, or very little effect at all. One might most confidently predict the former.

There are, however, increasing signs of a rather worrying trend to merger, which has recently grown apace. Over 1985—6, United bought Pan Am's Pacific network, Northwest Orient bought Republic, TWA was substantially restructured, Texas Air bought Eastern, People Express and Frontier. Not only does this activity lead to increasing concentration on specific routes, it may also herald an era of far less vigorous competition, if not implicit cartel behaviour. Late in 1986, United raised all its fares substantially and the others followed suit (*Economist*, 1 November 1986, p. 19).

In consequence, the eventual benefits of deregulation may be smaller, rather than larger, than industry analysts predicted in the mid 1980s.[10] This will depend, at least in part, upon the Justice Department's view of future mergers (currently, they do not have jurisdiction) and upon the success of any attempts to remove the effects of barriers to entry. Prime among these is the problem of access — access to slots at airports and access to travel agents' computer reservation systems. These systems, sponsored by powerful carriers, present information in a manner biased towards the system supplier.

What does all this suggest concerning the potential effects of airline deregulation in Europe? Here any remarks must be very speculative. First there would probably be a reduction in fares on balance. However, this may not be dramatic for at least three reasons. Distances in Europe are short, on average, and routes are mostly lightly trafficked. Also, the charter firms have a large slice of the lower end of the market, far more so than in the United States. The *Economist* article cited earlier suggests an average 15–20 per cent fall might be envisaged. Predictions concerning service changes and network developments would be rather too difficult to make.

The other moot point is the extent of political will in Europe for deregulation, and hence the degree of deregulation that would be likely to occur. Here it must be said that privatization of state carriers runs into fundamental conflict with deregulation. The value of the shares in the privatized firm depends heavily on the routes it will supply, which can only be uncertain in a very deregulated environment. Indeed, the UK experience in the period leading up to privatization of British Airways has been very much one of consolidating profitable routes in BA's hands. Of the two policies, deregulation and privatization, deregulation may be the more socially desirable, but this may effectively be blocked by a government intent on the latter.

7.5 Concluding remarks

The main purpose of this chapter has been to superimpose some representative empirical examples upon the earlier theoretical material in an attempt to chart certain facets of the increasing trends towards privatization, liberalization and deregulation. The following, final, chapter draws out

---

[10]The claim of Bailey et al. that 'There seem to be few incentives at present for domestic mergers' (p. 179) is outdated two years after publication!

some lessons from this and earlier material, using a rather broader perspective than hitherto.

Notes on the literature

A good general discussion of some of the issues and the semantics involved is provided by Kay and Silberston (1984), though note that their definitions differ in that they do not make my distinction between liberalization and deregulation. See also Beesley and Littlechild (1983). On public vs private, the surveys already cited, Borcherdling et al. (1982) and Yarrow (1986), together with Millward (1982) and Domberger and Piggott (1986), give fair coverage of issues and empirics. Entry generally is discussed in industrial economics/organization textbooks (e.g. Waterson, 1984a), but often not from the standpoint desired here. The telecommunications CPE area currently is still in a state of flux, and recommendations would be premature.

As regards contestability theory, the paper by Baumol and Willig (1986), read together with Schwartz (1986), provides an up-to-date account. A useful source on airline deregulation is Meyer's (1986) review of Bailey et al., but again, more material may be forthcoming. Joskow and Schmalensee (1983) provide an exploratory investigation of electricity deregulation. Lastly, most issues of *Fiscal Studies* in the period 1984 to 1987 have contained readily accessible papers of interest to the student of these debates in the UK context, papers for example on express coach deregulation (on which see also Button, 1985), and on the electricity industry.

8

A Summary Review

The problem of controlling natural monopoly is scarcely a new one. Indeed, Schmalensee (1979) has traced the origins of franchise bidding as far back as the mid-19th century in France, whilst state ownership goes back at least to the 1840 'penny post' of Rowland Hill in Britain, and Britain's railways were arguably a regulated form of transport as a result of the 1844 Regulation of Railways Act, which among other things specified some fares. It is also clear that economically acceptable, let alone politically acceptable, solutions are not easy to find. Various experiments such as municipal socialism, rate regulation and nationalization have been tried, and all have been found wanting to some extent.

Awareness of this historical context is important because there do appear to be certain fashions which take precedence from time to time. Currently, the fashion is very much towards privatization, with a secondary trend to deregulation. As the *Economist* put it, 'State-owned fossils are being carted off into the private sector almost everywhere' (23 February 1985, p. 15). The range of countries and of industries affected is staggering. Of course these are not all natural monopoly industries, but such trends can lead to a belief in a universal panacea which is bound to be disappointed. We shall return to this theme after reviewing some of the arguments presented earlier in the book.

8.1 Reviewing the arguments

Whether or not an industry is a natural monopoly is not an immutable fact. Technology and tastes (demand) are the fundamental influences, and as these change, optimal industry organization can change; industries which once were in this category may be removed from it, and new industries may become natural monopolies. To take two examples, when low-cost transmission of power around the UK became technically feasible, the concept of a national grid with natural monopoly features was created and local systems eventually became nationally controlled. On the other hand, if demand for airline services between two points increases greatly, the supply of such services can turn from being a natural monopoly (perhaps to a natural duopoly).

In a natural monopoly, it is most efficient for one firm to be the producer. Nevertheless, this does not mean it is impossible for a firm successfully to enter a natural monopoly market that is being run efficiently, if the entrant is able to choose a segment of the market to supply. Hence, restrictions on entry can be justified in some cases. To put it in a one-product firm context, average costs can start to rise without its being socially desirable for there to be more than one producer, because of the extra costs this would entail. Yet an entrant could offer restricted output at a lower average cost than the efficient incumbent natural monopolist, so destroying the economies. This point has another ramification — marginal cost pricing does not necessarily involve the firm making a loss; when average cost is rising, marginal cost exceeds it. Hence, desirable pricing policies do not necessarily imply exchequer funding and perpetual losses.

Despite what has been said above regarding restrictions on entry, the general view must be that both potential and actual entry are powerful constraining forces, particularly entry into sideline activities. An illustration is provided by the effects of liberalization of the supply of telephone peripherals such as answering machines, where prices have fallen sharply. Such constraining forces, in the absence of problems identified in the previous paragraph, improve efficiency, and indeed natural monopolies subject to easy entry are forced to be efficient.

Of course, many natural monopoly industries are not in fact ones in which entry, even if allowed, is easy. Entry often involves very substantial expenditure, much of which would not be returnable if the project were to fail. For example, a potential supplier of water to a particular area would have to engage in earthworks whose alternative uses would be very meagre. In such cases entry may not be attracted into the industry even if the incumbent firm is grossly inefficient, as long as it has some hold either on customers or over the necessary resources for supply.

Why might state-owned concerns be prone to inefficiency? Any firm is potentially inefficient if its managers are not supplied with clear objectives and are not subject to close constraints. The objectives, in the case of a state-owned concern, have either to be given explicitly, or supplied implicitly via financial controls, for example on investment. It is not enough to ask that the business be run efficiently, because this does not determine its size nor its product composition. Ownership cannot be equated with control.

It is important to note that state-owned concerns come under fewer natural constraints than do most private ones — this even includes rate regulated firms. Managers of privately owned firms are constrained by capital markets in ways that those in state-owned firms are not. The constraints include the threats (which no doubt may be impotent in particular cases) by shareholders to usurp current managers, by takeover raiders to capture the firm and by banks to call in receivers.

More importantly, perhaps, managers of private firms are also subject to what is called the managerial labour market constraint. A manager who is seen to have done badly is unlikely to get as good a job next time. Hence it has been argued that managers will discipline themselves partly in order to improve their career prospects, and indeed, discipline those immediately above and below them in the firm's hierarchy, so as to avoid negative effects on themselves. Such disciplining behaviour will happen in state-owned concerns only to the same extent if state firms fish in the same pool of managerial talent. That is to say, if people do not move between private and public industry, different behaviour patterns and work effort can be expected from the two sets of managers, and those in the state concerns are likely to exhibit worse performance.

Employees in state-owned concerns *may* feel more desire to cooperate with management (given similar jobs at equivalent pay levels), since there is no sense in which shareholder gains are made at workers' expense, but such increased cooperation need not be forthcoming in practice.

State control, then, is problematic. Yet most forms of rate regulation also suffer from potentially severe problems. The regulators have incentives to maintain and enhance their control, and maybe to allow the industry to develop in relatively inefficient ways. Moreover, the methods of regulation employed are quite likely to involve inbuilt inefficiencies such as incentives for the company to over-extend its capital stock, or to practise pricing distortions between their various products. And almost undoubtedly, the regulators will not be over-keen on a rapid rate of technical change in the industry if that leads to uncertainty concerning their position.

It is true that in some rather narrowly defined circumstances, franchise bidding may provide the way out of the control dilemma by introducing competition 'for the field'. However, this is conditional upon contracts being easily designed, specifications straightforwardly evaluated and firms held to their promises. The chequered record of defence contracting shows how important such caveats are.

Despite these rather negative remarks about state-owned, rate regulated and franchise bidding concerns, it is important to recognize their potential strengths. For example, a state-owned natural monopoly which is efficiently run and which is not out to milk consumers will be socially more desirable than a privately owned firm which is out to make high profits. It is important to recognize that the question of control structures is very much one of comparative institutions, all imperfect. In this context, unfettered private monopoly should be seen as one of these institutions.

8.2 Lessons for policy

From the economist's point of view, the focus in designing a policy should be pragmatism and efficiency rather than dogma. One structure is unlikely to suit the whole range of important natural monopoly institutions within the economy. These considerations condition the remarks that follow.

The first point to be made, given the earlier remarks about the current fashion towards privatization, is one endorsed by a broad spectrum of economists. Governments should understand that privatization of itself may do little to help the consumer, in the absence of measures to increase competition whenever such measures are possible. Here it would be remiss not to note that the privatization of British Gas in the UK in 1986 has been accompanied by remarkably little in the way of measures to induce competition where it is feasible, and that such measures as were incorporated essentially came through backbench (and Opposition) pressure on the government.

Competition can be introduced either at the point of privatization, or indeed in its absence, or through antitrust measures designed to ensure that the dominant firm does not succeed in any attempts to stifle potential opposition. Thus it can cogently be argued that privatization should be accompanied by a strengthening of antitrust legislation, so that competition is allowed to flourish where it can.

If we move outside the realm of privatization, we should note that there are several important changes that can be made to improve the efficiency of nationalized concerns, changes that may indeed make privatization irrelevant. One such key change may be to influence their managerial labour markets. For example, the present UK government's move away from pay being determined by Civil Service style 'top people' reviews, with their inevitable delays in salary rises, is probably welcome. The general point is that to many of the best potential managers (if not to their masters), a competitive salary is important. More specifically, efficiency criteria influencing the pay to top management can and should be introduced. There is no need to base these solely upon firms' financial performance factors, when there are available productivity and other qualitative efficiency measures of performance. Because it is social rather than private returns in which the state is interested, the most efficient performance will in general not be the most profitable. This point is relevant also to some forms of regulated firm. Of course market-determined salaries create some envy, but this is a penalty of attempting to get greater efficiency which it may be worthwhile to bear.

Another key factor in enhancing efficiency is to introduce more relevant and more potent watchdogs ('shareholders') or representatives of the public. Many issues are of local importance and cannot be properly appreciated at a national level, so that the use of local and democratic representation and influence seems desirable. Indeed, it was natural in the days of municipal utilities. Public criticism is best channelled to productive ends.

In addition, it is not beyond the wit of a man to develop incentive mechanisms that engender a positive attitude to technical change by both management and workforce. If a reorganization improves social efficiency, it ought to be possible to ensure that no affected group is disadvantaged by its adoption. Such reorganization should in principle encompass changes in management structures where these have become outmoded.

Additionally, 'efficiency audit' provisions such as those in the UK Competition Act 1980 are probably well worth retaining, together with the commitment to regular review of some aspects of the major state-owned concerns and the continued development of productivity indicators. In addition to the direct effects, the expertise gained by Monopolies Commission members in investigating private industry practices can be seen as relevant to making suggestions to public industries, in effect by strengthening the signals to the managerial labour market.

Moving briefly on to rate regulated firms, experiments with methods of regulation which are alternatives to rates of return are probably very desirable. Such alternatives as are used to regulate British Telecom and British Gas in the UK are probably in too early a stage to make evaluation possible, but given the manifold problems of rate regulation, they are likely to provide some useful lessons for future policy design.

Similarly, it will most likely be discovered that franchise bidding schemes operate better in some cases than others, and these experiments will be beneficial if they help to suggest what sorts of factors make franchising a success and in which areas it is likely to run into problems.

Finally, it is almost certain that current policy trends, like so many that have gone before, will at some stage succumb to a pendulum swing in the other direction as problems in policies such as privatization become apparent. This is particularly likely in the case of such policies without a coherent rationale, which independent observers have argued is the case with current UK privatization of natural monopolies (Bailey, 1986). The problem then is to see what aspects of the policy are worth retaining.

References

de Alessi, L. (1974) 'An economic analysis of government ownership and regulation: theory and evidence from the electric power industry', *Public Choice*, 19, 1−42.

de Alessi, L. (1977) 'Ownership and peak-load pricing in the electric power industry', *Quarterly Review of Economics and Business*, 17, 7−26.

Aoki, M. (1983) 'Managerialism revisited in the light of bargaining-game theory', *International Journal of Industrial Organisation*, 1, 1−21.

Arrow, K.J. (1984) 'The economics of agency', Technical report no. 451, Centre for Research on Organisational Efficiency, Stanford University.

Averch, H. and Johnson, L.L. (1962) 'Behaviour of the firm under regulatory constraint', *American Economic Review*, 52, 1053−69.

Bailey, E.E. (1973) *Economic Theory of Regulatory Constraint*, Lexington, Mass.: D.C. Heath.

Bailey, E.E. (1986) 'Price and productivity change following deregulation: the US experience', *Economic Journal*, 96, 1−17.

Bailey, E.E. and Friedlaender, A.F. (1982) 'Market structure and multi-product industries', *Journal of Economic Literature*, 20, 1024−48.

Bailey, E.E., Graham, D.R. and Kaplan, D.P. (1985) *Deregulating the Airlines*. Cambridge, Mass.: MIT Press.

Bain, J.S. (1956) *Barriers to New Competition*. Cambridge, Mass.: Harvard University Press.

Baker, C.A. (1915) 'Load factor, output and cost', *The Electrical Review*, 76, 775−7, 808−10, 841−3.

Baron, D.P. and Myerson, R.B. (1982) 'Regulating a monopolist with unknown costs', *Econometrica*, 50, 911−30.

Baron, D.P. and Taggart, R.A. (1977) 'A model of regulation under uncertainty and a test of regulatory bias', *Bell Journal of Economics*, 8, 151−67.

Baumol, W.J. (1959) *Business Behaviour, Value and Growth*. New York: Macmillan.

Baumol, W.J. (1984) 'Toward a theory of public enterprise', *Atlantic Economic Journal*, 12, 13−19.

Baumol, W.J. and Bradford, D.F. (1970) 'Optimal departures from marginal cost pricing', *American Economic Review*, 60, 265−83.

Baumol, W.J. and Klevorick, A.K. (1970) 'Input choices and rate-of-return regulation: an overview of the discussion', *Bell Journal of Economics*, 1, 162−90.

Baumol, W.J. and Willig, R.D. (1986) 'Contestability: developments since the book', *Oxford Economic Papers*, 38, Suppl., 9−36.

Baumol, W.J., Bailey, E.E. and Willig, R.D. (1977) 'Weak invisible hand

References

151

theorems on the sustainability of multiproduct natural monoply', *American Economic Review*, 67, 350–65.

Baumol, W.J., Panzar, J.C. and Willig, R.D. (1982) *Contestable Markets and the Theory of Industry Structure*. San Diego, Ca: Harcourt, Brace, Jovanovich.

Baumol, W.J., Panzar, J.C. and Willig, R.D. (1983) 'Contestable markets: an uprising in the theory of market structure: reply', *American Economic Review*, 73, 491–6.

Beesley, M.E. (1965) 'The value of time spent travelling: some new evidence', *Economica*, 32, 174–85.

Beesley, M. and Littlechild, S. (1983) 'Privatisation: principles, problems and priorities', *Lloyds Bank Review*, July, 1–20.

Berle, A.A. and Means, G.C. (1932) *The Modern Corporation and Private Property*. New York: Commerce Clearing House.

Boadway, R.W. and Bruce, N. (1984) *Welfare Economics*. Oxford: Basil Blackwell.

Borcherdling, T.E., Pommerehne, W.W. and Schneider, F. (1982) 'Comparing the efficiency of private and public production: the evidence from five countries', *Zeitschrift für Nationalökonömie*, Suppl. 2, 127–56.

Bös, D. (1986) *Public Enterprise Economics: Theory and Application*. Amsterdam: North Holland.

Brannan, L., Klein, J.D. and Weiss, L.N. (1984) 'Concentration and winning bids in auctions', *Antitrust Bulletin*, 29, 27–31.

Brock, W.A. (1984) 'Contestable markets and the theory of industry structure: a review article', *Journal of Political Economy*, 91, 1055–66.

Brown, I. (1986) 'The regulation of gas and electric utilities in the USA' (Lessons from America no. 5). London: Association for the Conservation of Energy.

Brown, S.J. and Sibley, D.S. (1986) *The Theory of Public Utility Pricing*. Cambridge: Cambridge University Press.

Button, K.J. (1985) 'New approaches to the regulation of industry', *Royal Bank of Scotland Review*, September, 18–34.

Byatt, I. (1984) 'The framework of government control', in Grieve-Smith (ed.) ch. 3.

Cable, J., Carruth, A. and Dixit, A. (1982) 'Conduct, structure and relative welfare losses in quantity-setting duopoly', 9th EARIE Conference Proceedings, 1, 296–324. Leuven, Belgium.

Callen, J., Matherson, G.F. and Mohring, H. (1976) 'The benefits and costs of rate of return regulation', *American Economic Review*, 66, 290–7.

Carlton, D.W., Landes, W. and Posner, R. (1980) 'Benefits and costs of airline mergers: a case study', *Bell Journal of Economics*, 11, 65–83.

Carsberg, B. (1986) 'Report of the Director General of telecommunications for the period 1 January to 31 December 1985', House of Commons paper 461, Session 1985/86. London: HMSO.

Caves, D.W. and Christensen, L.R. (1980) 'The relative efficiency of public and private firms in a competitive environment: the case of Canadian railroads', *Journal of Political Economy*, 88, 958–76.

Clarke, R. and McGuinness, T. (eds) (1987) *The Economics of the Firm*. Oxford: Basil Blackwell.

Clarkson, K.W. and Miller, R.L. (1982) *Industrial Organisation: Theory, Evidence and Public Policy*. London: McGraw Hill.

Cooper, R. and Ross, T.W. (1985) 'Product warranties and double moral hazard', *Rand Journal of Economics*, 16, 103–13.

Coursey, D., Isaac, R.M., Luke, M. and Smith, V.L. (1984) 'Market contestability in the presence of sunk (entry) costs', *Rand Journal of Economics*, 15, 69–84.

Crew, M.A. (1979) *Problems in Public Utility Economics and Regulation*. Lexington, Mass.: Lexington Books.

Crew, M.A., Jones-Lee, M.W. and Rowley, C.K. (1971) 'X-theory versus management discretion theory', *Southern Economic Journal*, 38, 173–84.

Curwen, P. (1986) *Public Enterprise: a Modern Approach*. Brighton: Wheatsheaf.

Danielsen, A.L. and Kamerschen, D.R. (eds) (1983) *Current Issues in Public-Utility Economics*. Lexington, Mass.: Lexington Books.

Das, S.P. (1980) 'On the effect of rate of return regulation under uncertainty', *American Economic Review*, 70, 456–60.

Daughety, A.F. (1984) 'Regulation and industrial organisation', *Journal of Political Economy*, 92, 932–55.

Deaton, A. and Muellbauer, J. (1980) *Economics and Consumer Behaviour*. Cambridge: Cambridge University Press.

Demsetz, H. (1968) 'Why regulate utilities?', *Journal of Law and Economics*, 11, 55–65.

Demski, J.S. (1976) 'Uncertainty and evaluation based on controllable performance', *Journal of Accounting Research*, 14, 230–45.

Diamond, P.A. (1971) 'A model of price adjustment', *Journal of Economic Theory*, 3, 156–68.

Director General of Fair Trading (1980) Annual report for the period January 1979 to December 1979, House of Commons Paper 624, Session 1979/80. London: HMSO.

Dixit, A.K. (1979) 'A model of duopoly suggesting a theory of entry barriers', *Bell Journal of Economics*, 10, 20–32.

Dixit, A.K. (1982) 'Recent developments in oligopoly theory', *American Economic Review*, papers and proceedings 72, 12–17.

Domberger, S., Meadowcroft, S.A. and Thompson, D.J. (1986) 'Competition, tendering and efficiency: the case of refuse collection', *Fiscal Studies*, 7, 69–84.

Domberger, S. and Middleton, J. (1985) 'Franchising in practice: the case of independent television in the UK', *Fiscal Studies*, 6, 17–32.

Domberger, S. and Piggott, J. (1986) 'Privatisation policies and public enterprise: a survey', *Economic Record*, 62, 145–62.

Energy Committee (1986) 'First Report from the Energy Committee', House of Commons Paper 15, Session 1985/6. London: HMSO.

Evans, D.S. and Heckman, J.J. (1984) 'A test for subadditivity of the cost function with an application to the Bell system', *American Economic Review*, 74, 615–23.

Fama, E.F. (1980) 'Agency problems and the theory of the firm', *Journal of Political Economy*, 88, 286–307.

Fama, E.F. and Jensen, M.C. (1983a) 'Separation of ownership and control', *Journal of Law and Economics*, 26, 301–25.

Fama, E.F. and Jensen, M.C. (1983b) 'Agency problems and residual claims', *Journal of Law and Economics*, 26, 327–49.

Faulhaber, G. (1975) 'Cross-subsidisation: pricing in public enterprises', *American Economic Review*, 65, 966–77.

Finsinger, J. (1983) 'Competition, ownership and control in markets with imperfect information', in J. Finsinger (ed.), *Economic Analysis of Regulated Markets*, London: Macmillan.

Finsinger, J. and Vogelsang, I. (1981) 'Alternative institutional frameworks for price incentive mechanisms', *Kyklos*, 34, 388–404.

Finsinger, J. and Vogelsang, I. (1985) 'Strategic management behaviour under reward structures in a planned economy', *Quarterly Journal of Economics*, 100, 263–70.

Foreman-Peck, J. and Manning, D. (1986) 'Liberalisation as an industrial policy: the case of telecommunications manufacturing', *National Westminster Bank Quarterly Review*, November, 20–33.

Foreman-Peck, J. and Waterson, M. (1985) 'The comparative efficiency of public and private enterprise in Britain: Electricity generation between the World Wars', *Economic Journal* (Suppl.), 95, 83–95.

Forsyth, P.J. (1984) 'Airlines and airports: privatisation, competition and regulation', *Fiscal Studies*, 5, no. 1, 61–75.

French, K.R. and McCormick, R.E. (1984) 'Sealed bids, sunk costs and the process of competition', *Journal of Business*, 57, 417–41.

Friedlaender, A.F., Winston, C. and Wang, K. (1983) 'Costs, technology and productivity in the US automobile industry', *Bell Journal of Economics*, 14, 1–20.

Gist, P. and Meadowcroft, S.A. (1986) 'Regulating for competition: the newly liberalised market for private branch exchanges', *Fiscal Studies*, 7, 41–65.

Glaister, S. and Mulley, C. (1983) *Public Control of the British Bus Industry*. Aldershot: Gower.

Goldberg, V.P. (1977) 'Competitive bidding and the production of pre-contract information', *Bell Journal of Economics*, 8, 250–61.

Gravelle, H.S.E. (1977) 'Marginal cost pricing under rate of return financial targets', *Manchester School*, 45, 236–40.

Gravelle, H.S.E. (1981a) 'Incentives, efficiency and control in public firms', Queen Mary College, London, discussion paper no. 72.

Gravelle, H.S.E. (1981b) 'Optimal prices and rate of return constraints', Queen Mary College, London, discussion paper no. 74.

Gravelle, H.S.E. (1985) 'Reward structures in a planned economy: some difficulties', *Quarterly Journal of Economics*, 100, 271–8.

Gravelle, H.S.E. and Katz, E. (1976) 'Financial targets and X-efficiency in public enterprises', *Public Finance*, 31, 218–34.

Green, J. and Laffont, J. (1979) *Incentives in Public Decision Making*. Amsterdam: North Holland.

Grieve-Smith, J. (ed.) (1984) *Strategic Planning in Nationalised Industries*. London: Macmillan.

Hagen, K.P. (1979) 'Optimal pricing in public firms in an imperfect market economy', *Scandinavian Journal of Economics*, 81, 475–93.

Hammond, E., Helm, D. and Thompson, D. (1985) 'British gas: options for privatisation', *Fiscal Studies*, 6, no. 4, 1–20.

Hammond, E.M., Helm, D.R. and Thompson, D.J. (1986) 'Competition in energy supply: has the energy act failed?', *Fiscal Studies*, 7, no. 1, 11–32.

Harlow, C. (1977) *Innovation and Productivity under Nationalisation*. London: Allen and Unwin.

Harrison, G.W. and McKee, M. (1985) 'Monopoly behaviour, decentralised regulation and contestable markets: an experimental evaluation', *Rand Journal of Economics*, 16, 51–69.

Hartley, K. and Huby, M. (1986) 'Contracting-out policy: theory and evidence', in Kay *et al.* (eds).

Hausman, W.J. and Neufeld, J.L. (1984) 'Time of day pricing in the US electric power industry at the turn of the century', *Rand Journal of Economics*, 15, 116–26.

Heald, D. (1980) 'The economic and financial control of the UK nationalised industries', *Economic Journal*, 90, 243–65.
Henney, A. (1984) 'Nationalised industry boards: how to make part-time members more effective', *Public Money*, 4, 47–50.
Hilton, G.W. (1972) 'The basic behaviour of regulatory commissions', *American Economic Review*, papers and proceedings 62, 47–54.
Jensen, M.C. and Meckling, W.H. (1976) 'Theory of the firm: managerial behaviour, agency costs and ownership structure'. *Journal of Financial Economics*, 3, 305–60.
Johnson, L.L. (1973) 'Behaviour of the firm under regulatory constraint: a reassessment', *American Economic Review*, papers and proceedings 63, 90–7.
Jones, T.T. and O'Brien, P.M. (1982) 'The composition, background and salaries of board members of nationalised industries with some private sector comparisons', UMIST, Department of Management Sciences, working paper no. 8211.
Joskow, P.L. and Noll, R.G. (1983) 'Regulation in theory and practice: an overview', in G. Fromm (ed.), *Studies in Public Regulation*, Cambridge, Mass.: MIT Press.
Joskow, P.L. and Schmalensee, R. (1983) *Markets for Power: an Analysis of Electric Utility Deregulation*. Cambridge, Mass.: MIT Press.
Kafoglis, M.Z. (1983) 'Regulatory lag in an inflationary environment', in Danielsen and Kamerschen (eds) ch. 13.
Kay, J., Mayer, C. and Thompson, D. (eds) (1986) *Privatisation and Regulation: the UK Experience*. Oxford: Clarendon Press.
Kay, J.A. and Silberston, Z.A. (1984) 'The new industrial policy — privatisation and competition', *Midland Bank Review*, Spring, 8–16.
Kay, J.A. and Thompson, D.J. (1986) 'Privatisation: a policy in search of a rationale', *Economic Journal*, 96, 18–32.
Klein, B., Crawford, R.G. and Alchian, A.A. (1978) 'Vertical integration, appropriable rents and the competitive contracting process', *Journal of Law and Economics*, 21, 297–326.
Kolbe, A.L. and Read, J.A. (Jr) (1984) *The Cost of Capital: Estimating the Rate of Return for Public Utilities*. Cambridge, Mass.: MIT Press.
Lambert, R.A. and Larcker, D.F. (1985) 'Executive compensation, corporate decision-making and shareholder wealth: a review of the evidence', *Midland Corporate Finance Journal*, 2, 6–22.
Leibenstein, H. (1966) 'Allocative efficiency vs. "X-efficiency"', *American Economic Review*, 56, 392–415.
Leland, H.E. and Meyer, R.A. (1976) 'Monopoly pricing structures with imperfect discrimination', *Bell Journal of Economics*, 5, 125–44.
Lewis, N. (1975) 'IBA programme contract awards', *Public Law*, 317–40.
Lewis, T.R. (1986) 'Reputation and contractual performance in long-term projects', *Rand Journal of Economics*, 17, 141–57.
Likierman, A. (1984) 'The impact of financial constraints', in Grieve-Smith (ed.), ch. 4.
Littlechild, S.C. (1986) *Economic Regulation of Privatised Water Authorities*. London: HMSO (for the Department of the Environment).
Loeb, M. and Magat, W.A. (1979) 'A decentralised method for utility regulation', *Journal of Law and Economics*, 22, 399–404.

Mankiw, G.B. and Whinston, M.D. (1986) 'Free entry and social inefficiency', *Rand Journal of Economics*, 17, 48–58.

McDonald, I.M. and Solow, R.M. (1981) 'Wage bargaining and employment', *American Economic Review*, 71, 896–908.

McGuinness, T. (1987) 'Markets and managerial hierarchies', in Clarke and McGuinness (eds), ch. 3.

Meyer, J.R. (1986) 'Bailey, Graham and Kaplan's *Deregulating the Airlines*', *Rand Journal of Economics*, 17, 461–6.

Millward, R. (1982) 'The comparative performance of public and private ownership', in E. Roll (ed.), *The Mixed Economy*, London: Macmillan.

Millward, R. and Ward, R. (1987) 'The comparative performance of public and private gas enterprises in the late nineteenth century', mimeo, University of Salford.

Mirman, L.J., Tauman, Y. and Zang, I. (1986) 'Ramsey prices, average cost prices and sustainability', *International Journal of Industrial Organisation*, 4, 123–40.

Mitchell, B.M. and Kleindorfer, P.R. (eds) (1980) *Regulated Industries and Public Enterprise*. Lexington, Mass.: Lexington Books.

Mitnick, B.M. (1980) *The Political Economy of Regulation*. New York: Columbia University Press.

Monopolies and Mergers Commission (1982) *Contraceptive Sheaths*. Cmnd 8689. London: HMSO.

Morrison, S. and Winston, C. (1986) *The Economic Effects of Airline Deregulation*. Washington DC: Brookings Institution.

Mueller, D.C. (ed.) (1980) *The Determinants and Effects of Mergers: an International Comparison*. Cambridge, Mass.: Oelschlager, Gunn and Hain.

Müller, J. (1986) 'Competition in the British telecommunications market: the impact of recent privatisation/deregulation decisions', mimeo, DIW, Berlin.

Nelson, R.A. and Wohar, M.E. (1983) 'Regulation, scale economies and productivity in steam-electric generation', *International Economic Review*, 24, 57–79.

Newbery, D.M. (1986) 'Energy policy issues after privatisation', Centre for Economic Policy Research, London, discussion paper no. 109.

Ng Y.-K. and Weisser, M. (1974) 'Optimal pricing with a budget constraint — the case of the two-part tariff', *Review of Economic Studies*, 41, 337–45.

Peacock, A.T. and Rowley, C.K. (1972) 'Welfare economics and the public regulation of natural monopoly', *Journal of Public Economics*, 1, 227–44.

Peles, Y.C. and Stein, J.L. (1986) 'The effect of rate of return regulation is highly sensitive to the nature of uncertainty', *American Economic Review*, 66, 278–89.

Peltzman, S. (1971) 'Pricing in public enterprises: electric utilities in the United States', *Journal of Law and Economics*, 14, 109–48.

Peltzman, S. (1976) 'Towards a more general theory of regulation', *Journal of Law and Economics*, 19, 211–40.

Perotin, V. and Estrin, S. (1986) 'Does ownership matter?', mimeo, London School of Economics.

Pescatrice, D.R. and Trapani, J.M. III (1980) 'The performance and objectives of public utilities operating in the United States', *Journal of Public Economics*, 13, 259–76.

Phillips, A. (1980) 'Ramsey pricing and sustainability with interdependent demands', in Mitchell and Kleindorfer (eds), ch. 10.

Posner, R.A. (1972) 'The appropriate scope of regulation in the cable television industry', *Bell Journal of Economics*, 3, 98−129.

Posner, R.A. (1974) 'Theories of economic regulation', *Bell Journal of Economics*, 5, 335−58.

Posner, R.A. (1975) 'The social costs of monopoly and regulation' *Journal of Political Economy*, 83, 807−27.

Prowse, M. (1986) 'Why ownership is not everything', *Financial Times*, 24 April

Pryke, R. (1981) *The Nationalised Industries: Policies and Performance since 1968*. Oxford: Martin Robertson.

Redwood, J. and Hatch, J. (1982) *Controlling Public Industries*. Oxford: Basil Blackwell.

Rees, R. (1968) 'Second-best rules for public enterprise pricing', *Economica*, 35, 260−73.

Rees, R. (1984) *Public Enterprise Economics*, 2nd edn. London: Weidenfeld and Nicolson.

Samuelson, W.F. (1985) 'Competitive bidding with entry costs', *Economics Letters*, 17, 53−7.

Saving, T.R. (1982) 'Market organisation and product quality', *Southern Economic Journal*, 48, 855−67.

Schmalensee, R. (1979) *The Control of Natural Monopolies*, Lexington, Mass.: D.C. Heath.

Schmalensee, R. (1982) 'Another look at market power', *Harvard Law Review*, 95, 1789−816.

Schwartz, M. (1986) 'The nature and scope of contestability theory', *Oxford Economic Papers*, 38, Suppl., 37−57.

Schwartz, M. and Reynolds, R.J. (1983) 'Contestable markets: an uprising in the theory of industry structure: comment', *American Economic Review*, 73, 488−90.

Sendall, B. (1982) *Independent Television in Britain:* vol. 1, *Origins and Foundation 1946−63*, London: Macmillan.

Sharkey, W.W. (1982) *The Theory of Natural Monopoly*. Cambridge: Cambridge University Press.

Shavell, S. (1979) 'Risk sharing and incentives in the principal and agent relationship', *Bell Journal of Economics*, 10, 55−73.

Shaw, R.W. (1974) 'Price leadership and the effect of new entry on the UK retail petrol supply market', *Journal of Industrial Economics*, 23, 65−79.

Shepherd, W.G. (1984) 'Contestability vs. competition', *American Economic Review*, 74, 572−87.

Shleifer, A. (1985) 'A theory of yardstick competition', *Rand Journal of Economics*, 16, 319−27.

Smirlock, M. and Marshall, W. (1983) 'Monopoly power and expense preference behaviour: theory and evidence to the contrary', *Bell Journal of Economics*, 14, 166−78.

Spence, A.M. (1975) 'The economics of internal organisation: an introduction', *Bell Journal of Economics*, 6, 163−72.

Spence, A.M. (1976) 'Product differentiation and welfare', *American Economic Review*, papers and proceedings 66, 407–14.
Stelzer, I. (1983) 'Franchising cable TV: how the US got it wrong', *Public Money*, 3, 49–52.
Stigler, G.J. (1964) 'A theory of oligopoly', *Journal of Political Economy*, 72, 44–61.
Stigler, G.J. (1971) 'The theory of economic regulation', *Bell Journal of Economics*, 2, 3–21.
Stigler, G.J. (1975) *The Citizen and the State: Essays on Regulation.* Chicago, Ill.: University of Chicago Press.
Stiglitz, J.E. (1979) 'Equilibrium in product markets with imperfect information', *American Economic Review*, 69, 339–45.
Stiglitz, J.E. (1985) 'Credit markets and the control of capital', *Journal of Money, Credit and Banking*, 17, 133–52.
Strong, N. and Waterson, M. (1987) 'Principals, agents and information', in Clarke and McGuinness (eds), ch. 2.
Tam, M.-Y.S. (1985) 'Reward structures in a planned economy: some further thoughts', *Quarterly Journal of Economics*, 100, 279–90.
Telser, L. (1969) 'On the regulation of industry: a note', *Journal of Political Economy*, 77, 937–52.
Thompson, R.S. (1983) 'Diffusion of the M-form structure in the UK: rate of imitation, inter-firm and inter-industry differences', *International Journal of Industrial Organisation*, 1, 297–315.
Tomlinson, J.D. (1983) Regulating the capitalist enterprise: the impossible dream?', *Scottish Journal of Political Economy*, 30, 54–68.
TUC (1984) *Contractors' Failures: the Privatisation Experience.* London: Trades Union Congress.
United States Department of Commerce (1985) National Telecommunications and Information Administration. *Competition Benefits Reports*, Washington DC.
Varian, H.R. (1978) *Microeconomic Analysis.* New York: Norton.
Veljanovski, C.G. and Bishop, W.D. (1983) *Choice by Cable.* Institute for Economic Affairs, London, Hobart paper 96.
Vernon, J.M. and Graham, D.A. (1971) 'Profitability of monopolisation by vertical integration', *Journal of Political Economy*, 79, 924–5.
Vickers, J. and Yarrow, G. (1985) *Privatisation and the Natural Monopolies.* London: Public Policy Centre.
Vogelsang, I. (1986) 'Two-part tariffs as regulatory constraints', mimeo, Boston, Mass.
Waterson, M. (1984a) *Economic Theory of the Industry.* Cambridge: Cambridge University Press.
Waterson, M. (1984b) 'Issues in the regulation of cable TV', *International Review of Law and Economics*, 4, 67–82.
Webb, M.G. (1980) 'A critical appraisal of United Kingdom policy for the nationalised industries', in Mitchell and Kleindorfer (eds), ch. 7.
Weitzman, M.L. (1977) 'Is the price system or rationing more effective in getting a commodity to those who need it most?', *Bell Journal of Economics*, 8, 517–24.

Weitzman, M.L. (1983) 'Contestable markets: an uprising in the theory of industry structure: comment', *American Economic Review*, 73, 486—7.

von Weizsäcker, C.C. (1980) 'A welfare analysis of barriers to entry', *Bell Journal of Economics*, 11, 399—420.

von Weizsäcker, C.C. (1984) 'Free entry into telecommunications?', in H. Giersch (ed.), *New Opportunities for Entrepreneurship*, Tubingen: Mohr-Verlag.

Wenders, J.T. (1986) 'The Economic Theory of Regulation and the US Telecommunications Industry', mimeo, Moscow, Idaho.

Williamson, O.E. (1963) 'Managerial discretion and business behaviour', *American Economic Review*, 53, 1032—57.

Williamson, O.E. (1975) *Markets and Hierarchies: Analysis and Antitrust Implications*. New York: Free Press.

Williamson, O.E. (1976) 'Franchise bidding for natural monopolies — in general and with respect to CATV', *Bell Journal of Economics*, 7, 73—104.

Willig, R.D. (1976) 'Consumers' surplus without apology', *American Economic Review*, 66, 589—97.

Willig, R.D. (1978) 'Pareto-superior non-linear outlay schedules', *Bell Journal of Economics*, 9, 56—69.

Wilson, J.Q. (ed.) (1980) *The Politics of Regulation*. New York: Basic Books.

Yarrow, G. (1986) 'Privatisation in theory and practice', *Economic Policy*, 1, 324—77.

Zajac, E.E. (1970) 'A geometric treatment of Averch—Johnson's behaviour of the firm model', *American Economic Review*, 60, 117—25.

Index

Fama, E.F. 8, 42, 43
Fama, E.F. and Jensen, M.C. 47, 48
Faulhaber, G. 34, 35
financial targets 80
financial mutuals 48
financial performance criteria 54
Finsinger, J. 48
Finsinger, J. and Vogelsang, I. 55, 76, 78, 83, 100
fixed costs 28, 31, 33−4, 137
Foreman-Peck, J. and Manning, D. 134
Foreman-Peck, J. and Waterson, M. 126
Forsyth, P.J. 44
franchise bidding *see* bidding schemes
free-rider problem 29, 40
French, K.R. and McCormick, R.E. 109
Friedlaender, A.F. et al. 37

gas industry 10−12, 66, 104
gas supply 127
GDP 12
Glaister, S. and Mulley, C. 124
Goldberg, V.P. 121
Golden Wonder 132
governmental intervention 1, 3
Gravelle, H.S.E. 71, 72, 75, 77, 78
Gravelle, H.S.E. and Katz, E. 74
Green, J. and Laffont, J. 23

Hagen, K.P. 66
Hammond, E. et al. 105
Hammond, E.M. et al. 127
Harlow, C. 83
Harrison, G.W. and McKee, M. 138
Hartley, K. and Huby, M. 128
Hausman, W.J. and Neufeld, J.L. 127
Heald, D. 79
Henney, A. 82
hidden action 52
hidden information 52
hidden knowledge 52, 57
Hilton, G.W. 12, 101
Hush-a-Phone 133

implicit contract theory 57

incentive mechanisms 99−101
incentive schemes 55−6, 76−7
incentive structure 39, 54, 77
income function, concave utility of 49
income redistributional measures 64
incomplete long-term contracts 115
institutional constraint structures 44
insurance 48, 51, 52
internal firm relationships 49−55
Interstate Communications Commission 7
invisible hand 63

Jensen, M.C. and Meckling, W.H 39
Johnson, L.L. 89, 105
Jones, T.T. and O'Brien, P.M. 81
Joskow, P.L. and Noll, R.G. 12
Joskow, P.L. and Schmalensee, R. 144

Kafoglis, M.Z. 89
Kay, J.A. and Silbertson, Z.A. 58, 144
Kay, J.A. and Thompson, D.J. 44, 58
Klein, B. et al. 121
Kolbe, A.L. and Read, J.A. 102
Kuhn−Tucker problem 86

Labour Party 10
Lagrangean function 23, 71, 85
Lagrangean multiplier technique 23
Laker Airways 131
Lambert, R.A. and Larcker, D.F. 58
Laspeyres cost index system 90
Leibenstein, H. 42
Leland, H.E. and Meyer, R.A. 70
Lewis, N. 120
Lewis, T.R. 112
liberalization 122−5, 133, 134−5
Likierman, A. 80
Lindahl pricing 23
liquidation 48
Littlechild, S.C. 95, 103, 105
load factor 141
Loeb, M. and Magat, W.A. 76, 139
loosening of regulatory control 122

McDonald, I.M. and Solow, R.M. 56

McGuinness, T. 58
management consultancy 81
manager–employee relationship
  55–7
managerial effort 77
managerial emoluments 49–55, 76
managerial incentive package 52–5,
  76, 81–2, 101
managerial labour market 42–4, 46,
  47, 147
managerial utility models 73–8
managers
  controls on 45
  of large private corporations 39
  peer group pressure on 42
Mankiw, G.B. and Whinston, M.D.
  130
marginal cost pricing 14, 18, 21,
  65–70
market factor price ratio 72
market failures 2, 12
market structure effects 58
Mercury 134
Meyer, J.R. 144
Milk Marketing Board 7
Millward, R. 127, 144
Millward, R. and Ward, R. 127
Ministry of International Trade and
  Industry 64
Mirman, L.J. et al. 35
Mitchell, B.M. and Kleindorfer, P.R.
  105
Mitel 134
Mitnick, B.M. 12
modelling of constraints and
  objectives 71–8
monopolies, public versus private 58,
  125–9
Monopolies (and Mergers) Commission 4, 6, 9, 81, 103, 149
monopoly welfare loss 11
moral hazard 51, 113
Morrison, S. and Winston, C. 140,
  141, 142
Mueller, D.C. 94
multidivisional (or M) form of
  organization 56
multiproduct costs 19
multiproduct subadditivity 25–6

nationalized industries 79–83
nationalized industry boards 81
natural monopoly 3, 4, 6, 10,
  13–37, 123, 125, 145, 146
  benchmark for evaluating 32–3
  definition 15, 16
  interpretations of term 15
  literature 37
  not sustainable 18
  single-product 15–19
  sustainable 30–1
  see also under subadditivity
Nelson, R.A. and Wohar, M.E. 135
'never knowingly undersold' strategy
  29
Newbery, D.M. 105
Ng, Y.-K. and Weisser, M. 69, 70
non-financial performance indicators
  80–1
nonlinear outlay schedules 23, 68
non-profit organizations 47
Northern Telecom 133

Office of Fair Trading 103
Oftel 103, 105
operating franchises 113–14

Pareto-optimal 14
partnerships 47, 48
Peacock, A.T. and Rowley, C.K. 13
peak load problem 67
peer group pressure on managers 42
Peltzman, S. 8, 127
perfect competition 2, 7, 42
perfect contestability 28, 30, 32–3,
  136–8
performance indicators 81
Perotin, V. and Estrin, S. 48, 82
Pescatrice, D.R. and Trapani, J.M. III
  126
Phillips, A. 68
planning, state 64
policy design 149
policy lessons 148
policy trends 149
political tradeoffs 78
politics and politicians 6, 8–9
Posner, R.A. 7, 8, 12, 107, 110,
  114, 119, 121